MOMENTS
of PEACE
for the
EVENING

PRESENTED TO

PRESENTED BY

DATE

MOMENTS
of PEACE
for the
EVENING

MOMENTS
of PEACE
for the
EVENING

BETHANYHOUSE

MINNEAPOLIS, MINNESOTA

Moments of Peace for the Evening
Copyright © 2005 by GRQ, Inc.
Brentwood, Tennessee 37027

Published by Bethany House Publishers
11400 Hampshire Avenue South
Bloomington, Minnesota 55438

Bethany House Publishers is a division of Baker Publishing Group, Grand Rapids, Michigan.

ISBN 0-7642-0170-0

Editor: Lila Empson
Associate Editor: Natasha Sperling
Writer: Jennifer Rosania
Design: Thatcher Design, Nashville, Tessessee

05 06 07   4 3 2 1

**We can understand these things,
for we have the mind of Christ.**

1 CORINTHIANS 2:16 NLT

CONTENTS

Introduction

Good evening. Thank you for ending your day with God.

Just as your body needs to rest each night in order to be renewed and healthy, so reflecting on the Bible will replenish your soul with grace and hope. There is nothing that will give you such a sustaining peace and satisfying slumber as seeking God and feeling his presence in the evening.

These brief meditations have been fashioned to help you reflect and to give you hope. Your faith will be strengthened, and you will be encouraged to live it out. And every evening you will experience the wonderful reassurance of God's power and kindness.

Undoubtedly, the Bible will guide you, God's grace will comfort you, and his love will give you tranquility as you close your eyes to sleep.

God is waiting to fill you with joy and to assure you that he is with you on every step of your journey. So read, pray, and enjoy your moments of grace each evening.

And may your nightly meetings with God completely bless your soul.

I think about you before I go to sleep, and
my thoughts turn to you during the night.
You have helped me, and I sing happy songs.
PSALM 63:6–7 CEV

Moments of Peace
for the Evening

May the God of hope fill you with all joy and peace in believing, that you may abound in hope.

ROMANS 15:13 NKJV

Beginning Anew

As you sit down with your Bible and this devotion tonight, what is it that you are seeking? Do you desire to return to God? Do you long for the peace that can only come from him? Do you need a fresh start?

God has initiated that longing within you and has drawn you to himself so that you can know his peace. He wants to give you a fresh start and love you lavishly. He wants to show you that all things can be new if you will allow him into your life.

> I will heal their waywardness. I will love them lavishly. My anger is played out. I will make a fresh start with Israel.
>
> HOSEA 14:4 MSG

God's mercy and peace are available to you tonight. Will you open your heart to him?

Dear God, I will open my heart to your lavish love. Thank you for drawing me to yourself, and for giving me a new beginning. Amen.

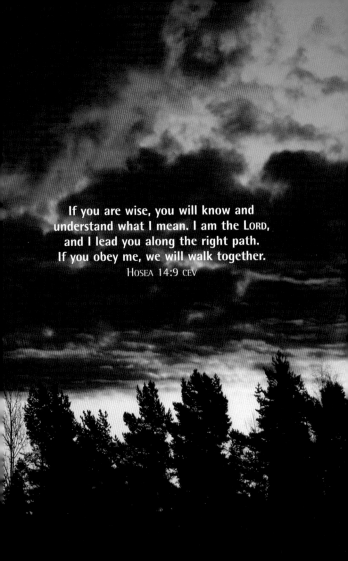

If you are wise, you will know and understand what I mean. I am the LORD, and I lead you along the right path. If you obey me, we will walk together.

HOSEA 14:9 CEV

Words of Peace

They were caught in an angry tempest of such violent intensity that even the seasoned fishermen were afraid for their lives. So they woke Jesus, who was somehow still sleeping, and implored his help.

He rose and rebuked the furious squall. Instantly, all grew calm.

Perhaps something in your day was like that battering storm and even now your heart is agitated, like a ship on the billowing sea. God can calm you with his gentle words and speak peace into your situation if you will allow him.

> **He arose and rebuked the winds and the sea, and there was a great calm.**
> MATTHEW 8:26 NKJV

So call out to him—pray and read the Bible. God will pacify your raging storm and bring tranquility to your heart. Rest in him tonight.

Dear God, thank you for speaking peace into my life. Truly it is astounding that even the winds and waves obey you. Amen.

The men were
stunned with
bewildered wonder
and marveled,
saying, What kind
of Man is this,
that even the
winds and the
sea obey Him!

MATTHEW 8:27 AMP

Filled With Hope

The word *filled* may not exactly portray your condition at the end of a day. Perhaps *drained* is a better description of how you have been emptied of energy, creativity, and even patience.

> **May the God of hope fill you with all joy and peace in believing, that you may abound in hope.**
>
> ROMANS 15:13 NKJV

Yet it is precisely when you have reached the end of your own resources that God begins to fill you with his. He shows you that he sufficiently supplies what you lack and satisfies your deepest yearnings.

It is his desire to fill you with hope—the knowledge that you will have joy and peace when you trust his help in every circumstance. So be filled with him tonight and rest easy. He will surely satisfy your soul.

Dear God, I am drained. However, I praise you because I know you will fill me with hope and help me in wonderful ways. Amen.

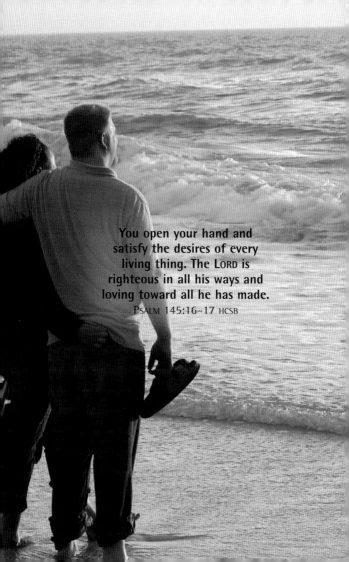

You open your hand and
satisfy the desires of every
living thing. The LORD is
righteous in all his ways and
loving toward all he has made.
PSALM 145:16–17 HCSB

Your Reliable Advocate

Change, even if it is positive, can be stressful. At times it will feel like everything is fluctuating—friends relocate, jobs come and go, and even values can vary with cultural trends. It can be difficult to make a decision when everything is so unpredictable.

> **Jesus Christ (the Messiah) is [always] the same, yesterday, today, [yes] and forever.**
> HEBREWS 13:8 AMP

However, the one thing you can hold on to when everything else is shifting is God. No matter what happened today—or what may occur tomorrow—he will never stop loving you, and he is always ready to help you.

Are things changing for you? Then you need an advocate that is wise and trustworthy. Tonight, rest easy knowing that God's reliable counsel and strength are available to you.

Dear God, tonight I want to thank you for never, ever changing. I praise you for being my reliable advocate in this unpredictable world. Amen.

The works of his hands are faithful and just; all his precepts are trustworthy; they are established forever and ever, to be performed with faithfulness and uprightness.

PSALM 111:7–8 ESV

A Private Discussion

It can be very lonely when you have private issues that you cannot share with others. Whether they are difficult to explain or your loved ones just wouldn't understand, keeping silent can make you feel isolated and discouraged.

> When you pray, go into your private room . . . and your Father who sees in secret will reward you.
>
> MATTHEW 6:6 HCSB

Yet there is one who already knows what you are experiencing, and his understanding and wisdom are more than sufficient. You can be honest with God because nothing is hidden from him.

Therefore, whatever you are facing, talk it out with God tonight—just plainly tell him how you feel. Then listen. You will find that having someone who loves you so much and whom you can talk to is a great reward.

Dear God, I need to talk to you about the things that concern me. Help me to be vulnerable—knowing that you love me and are fully trustworthy. Thank you for listening. Amen.

I call to you, God, and you
answer me. Listen to me
now, and hear what I say.

PSALM 17:6 NCV

An Understanding Helper

Sometimes the Bible will not make sense. You will easily comprehend the stories, but something about them will not connect. You will feel as if there were some point that is just beyond your reach.

It will be as if a voice within you were asking, *Do you understand this?*

This is God's spirit stretching you. He will bring the story or lesson back to your mind repeatedly in order to clarify a truth that you need to know.

Tonight, if there is some passage of the Bible that has you stumped, rejoice. It is probably a principle that God's spirit is trying to teach you in a special way.

Dear God, thank you for your spirit and for patiently explaining these wonderful truths. I praise you for being a wise and effective teacher. Amen.

We received
the Spirit
that is from
God so that
we can know
all that God
has given us.

1 Corinthians
2:12 NCV

Drying Your Tears

Have you been crying out to God about some dear person or situation tonight? Is there a promise you long for him to fulfill? God will surely be kind and loving to you, and you are absolutely assured that he is going to answer you.

> You will weep no more. He will surely be gracious to you at the sound of your cry; when He hears it, He will answer you.
> ISAIAH 30:19 AMP

In light of this, ask yourself: Is what draws your tears your own doubt that God will help you? Sometimes your tears are actually evidence that your trust in God must increase.

Take this to heart— God will never, ever fail you. So dry your tears tonight and embrace the peace he longs to give to you. Know that he is absolutely faithful to do as he promised.

Dear God, it is true that sometimes my faith is weak. Please help me trust in you more, for surely you are already answering my prayers. Amen.

I have sought your face with all my heart; be gracious to me according to your promise.

PSALM 119:58 NIV

The Never-Failing Source

Everyone has trouble persevering at one point or another. It may be difficult to continue physically because your body needs sleep, healing, and sustenance. Or perhaps it is your spirit that is struggling with decisions and worries that are too massive for you to handle.

> My flesh and my heart may fail, but God is the strength of my heart and my portion forever.
> PSALM 73:26 NASB

You may feel yourself slipping from a successful course because you've exhausted all of your resources. However, there is a source that will never fail to sustain you. God fortifies and encourages you in many ways.

Tonight, allow yourself to be weak so that God can be strong in you. Rely on God to be your never-failing source that leads you to victory.

Dear God, I thank you that nothing in my situation is too much for you. I praise you for sustaining me and being my portion forever. Amen.

It is God who arms me with strength and makes my way perfect.

2 Samuel 22:33 NIV

A Heavenly Conversation

If you had a problem in which you had limited knowledge—be it medical, legal, relational, mechanical, or other—you would probably find an expert to help you with it.

Depending on what that professional charged, you most likely would spend the meeting listening, making the most of their costly time.

> **Guard your steps as you go to the house of God, and draw near to listen.**
> ECCLESIASTES 5:1 NASB

This evening, there are important matters that you will take to God. Though you absolutely should express your feelings, consider this: God is an expert when it comes to everything concerning your life.

If you do all the talking, you will miss the life-giving counsel that you need. Therefore, when you pray tonight, make the most of your time with God by listening.

Dear God, I know you want to hear me, but I also want to hear you. Thank you for giving me the heavenly counsel I need. Amen.

God is in heaven, and you on earth;
therefore let your words be few.

ECCLESIASTES 5:2 NKJV

The Wonder of Modesty

Can you really deliver all that you've agreed to? This question will vex you whenever you make promises that are impossible to keep.

When you overestimate yourself to win the favor of others, you can become trapped and overextended to the point of exhaustion.

You have fallen into a snare, but you hold the key that unlocks it. All you must do is humbly admit to misjudging your abilities. Do not make excuses. Simply acknowledge that the task is more than you can handle.

> **If you have been trapped by what you said, ensnared by the words of your mouth . . . Go and humble yourself.**
> PROVERBS 6:2–3 NIV

The wonder of modesty is that others will relate to your vulnerability. They will think more highly of you because you are honest about yourself.

Dear God, keep me from overestimating my abilities. Rather, help me to be humble and under promise—so that others will be pleased when I over deliver. Amen.

With humility comes wisdom.

PROVERBS 11:2 HCSB

Steady on in Faith

How does one avoid being pitched by storm-driven waves? Surely a deep understanding of the ocean and a sturdy, seaworthy vessel are the best tools to combat the onslaught.

> **When you ask for something, you must have faith and not doubt. Anyone who doubts is like an ocean wave tossed around in a storm.**
> JAMES 1:6 CEV

The same is true for the person who desires to sail steady on in faith.

You know what it is to have the waves of what-ifs battering your trust in God's promises. Yet you also know that your storms of doubt are merely bluster and that you can learn to steer clear of them.

God is the strong vessel of your confidence. He carries you to your destination.

So tonight have faith. Enjoy the calm waters of believing in him completely.

Dear God, help me to realize when I am approaching a storm of doubt, so I can avoid it by putting my full faith in you. Amen.

He stilled the storm to a murmur, and the waves of the sea were hushed. They rejoiced when the waves grew quiet. Then He guided them to the harbor they longed for.

PSALM 107:29–30 HCSB

Dedicated and Obedient

The psalmist discovered the blessing of agreeing with God. To follow his instructions is to experience liberty and joy beyond what the heart can ever know on its own.

As orator and clergyman Henry Ward Beecher wrote, "The strength and happiness of a man consists in finding out the way in which God is going, and going in that way too."

> **Oh, that my actions would consistently reflect your principles!**
> PSALM 119:5 NLT

Not that it is ever easy—by any means. You will find it is challenging to practice his principles. However, if you are dedicated and obey him out of love, you will find that the way he is going leads to the destination you've always longed to reach.

Dear God, please help me to be dedicated and obedient to your principles so that I can learn your wonderful truth and follow wherever you go. Amen.

Be good to me, your servant, so that
I may live and obey your teachings.
Open my eyes, so that I may see the
wonderful truths in your law.

PSALM 119:17–18 GNT

Standing Firm

The armor of God consists of the belt of truth, the breastplate of right living, the shoes of good news, the shield of faith, the helmet of salvation, and the sword of the spirit—which is the Bible.

Obviously, the battles fought with these instruments are not engaged on conventional battlefields. Rather, they are provided for protection in the spiritual arena—for your thoughts, values, reputation, purpose, and even your trust in God.

> **Take up the whole armor of God, that you may be able to withstand in the evil day, and having done all, to stand.**
>
> EPHESIANS 6:13 NKJV

God safeguards your spirit completely—including your heart and mind. Cover yourself with truth, right living, salvation, faith, and the Bible. You will be able to stand firm no matter what conflicts may come.

Dear God, thank you for this amazing armor. I know you will keep my spirit strong and will help me to stand firm always. Amen.

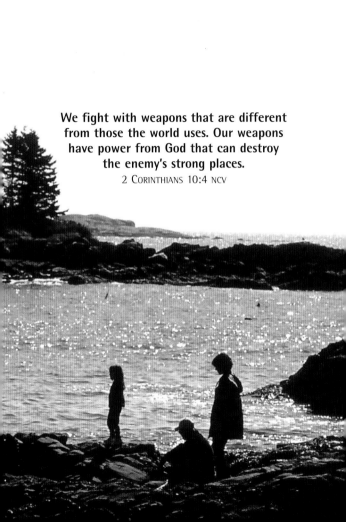

We fight with weapons that are different
from those the world uses. Our weapons
have power from God that can destroy
the enemy's strong places.

2 CORINTHIANS 10:4 NCV

Knowing His Promises

It is God's great promise to you—that dream you have in your heart that he has confirmed through prayer and the Bible. As the day draws to an end, you are reminded of how many suns have set without you seeing the promise fulfilled.

> **He has granted to us his precious and very great promises, so that through them you may become partakers of the divine nature.**
> 2 PETER 1:4 ESV

Why would God allow this lengthy delay? Because he grows you through it. As you wait, God reveals himself to you and builds his holiness, patience, hope, and confidence in you.

This evening, rejoice that you are not only gaining the promise but also gaining God's nature as well. In the end, you may even find that your true longing was for God all along.

Dear God, thank you that I will know you better through this waiting. However, I also praise you that I will soon see your promise fulfilled. Amen.

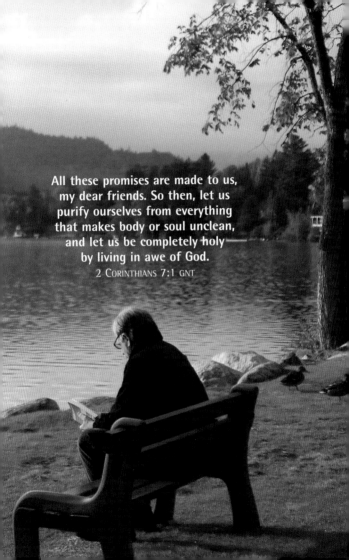

All these promises are made to us, my dear friends. So then, let us purify ourselves from everything that makes body or soul unclean, and let us be completely holy by living in awe of God.

2 CORINTHIANS 7:1 GNT

Moments of Peace
for the Evening

He has granted to us his precious and
very great promises, so that through
them you may become partakers of
the divine nature.

2 PETER 1:4 ESV

An Everlasting Purpose

Joshua spent years leading the people of Israel into the Promised Land. Then they were at the end of the journey, ready to cultivate the land they had conquered.

You may imagine that Joshua felt that his usefulness had come to an end. Yet through the journey, Joshua discovered that he had been created to love and obey God wherever he was. And he was committed to living out that purpose for the rest of his life.

> **Love the Lord your God, walk in all His ways, keep His commands, remain faithful to Him, and serve Him with all your heart and all your soul.**
> JOSHUA 22:5 HCSB

If you ever feel like you lack purpose, remember that you, too, were created to have a relationship with God. He made you in order to love you—and that is an excellent purpose.

Dear God, you created me to have a wonderful relationship with you. Help me love you and obey you every day of my life. Amen.

As for me and my house,
we will serve the Lord.

JOSHUA 24:15 NASB

An Abundance of Love

If you have to be in debt, it is good to owe love, of which you have an endless supply. You have an abundant source of love through God, who cares for you unconditionally and without limitation. And the more you spend his love, the more it multiplies.

> **Let no debt remain outstanding, except the continuing debt to love one another, for he who loves his fellowman has fulfilled the law.**
>
> ROMANS 13:8 NIV

As you reflect on your day, consider this: Have you been stingy in expressing your love? Is there someone who needs your kindness, but busyness has prevented you from showing that you care?

Draw from God's bank of love and make an investment into that person's life. Certainly, you will be as richly blessed in the giving as your friend is in the receiving.

Dear God, I can think of someone who needs your love. Help me to give it generously, and bless this person's life to your glory. Amen.

When we place our faith in Christ
Jesus . . . what is important is
faith expressing itself in love.

GALATIANS 5:6 NLT

A Sacrifice of Praise

It is not shocking that missionaries Paul and Silas were in prison—their preaching often angered the religious leaders. What was surprising, however, was their response to being beaten and chained. To everyone's amazement, they sang hymns to God.

> About midnight, Paul and Silas were at prayer and singing a robust hymn to God. The other prisoners couldn't believe their ears.
> ACTS 16:25 MSG

How do people praise God when they hurt? It is a difficult sacrifice, to be sure. However, it asserts the foundational belief that no matter what the situation, God holds the situation safely in his hands.

God freed Paul and Silas from prison, and he can release you from your pain as well. So sing a hymn of praise to him, and experience the way he honors your sacrifice.

Dear God, I praise you for being in control of every situation—especially this one. Thank you for setting me free. Amen.

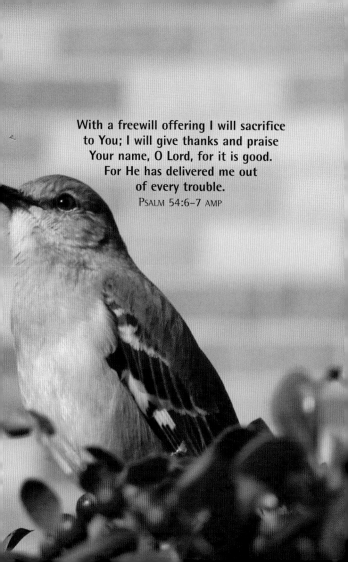

With a freewill offering I will sacrifice
to You; I will give thanks and praise
Your name, O Lord, for it is good.
For He has delivered me out
of every trouble.

PSALM 54:6–7 AMP

Overwhelmed by Awe

When the temple was completed, all the Israelites went to see it and praise God. They played their instruments, sang, and rejoiced. Then something amazing happened—God's glory appeared and filled the temple. It was so overwhelming that even the priests stopped what they were doing.

> **The priests could not continue their work because the glorious presence of the LORD filled the Temple of God.**
>
> 2 CHRONICLES 5:14
> NLT

Sometimes the presence of God will be so overpowering that it will stop you in your tracks. At those times, it is okay if you don't know what to do or say—because being in God's presence is all that really matters.

Never fear taking time to experience God. Just enjoy having him near.

Dear God, your brilliant beauty amazes me. I long for your overwhelming presence, and sit quietly to experience the full glory of my God. Amen.

Who among the gods is like you, O Lord?
Who is like you—majestic in holiness,
awesome in glory, working wonders?

EXODUS 15:11 NIV

Awaiting the Glory

This is the message for you this evening: Do not lose heart. Though pressures of the day have overwhelmed you, though dreams are long in being fulfilled, though you are physically and emotionally exhausted, embrace this hope.

We do not lose heart . . . for our light and momentary troubles are achieving for us an eternal glory that far out-weighs them all.

2 CORINTHIANS 4:16–17 NIV

When you receive God's magnificent promise, the troubles and fatigue you feel right now will seem light, momentary—and easily forgettable. You will see God's glory, and it will be the most extraordinary thing you've ever experienced.

Take courage this evening, and rejoice. Trust in God and eagerly expect him to work in your life. Surely you will have overwhelming joy when you finally see his glory.

Dear God, I cling to your promise and long to see your glory. I praise you for always strengthening me with your unshakable hope. Amen.

I hope in You, O LORD; You
will answer, O Lord my God
PSALM 38:15 NASB

Receiving Your Prayers

More than anything else in the world, Hannah wanted a baby. She often wept while she prayed because her desire for a child was so ingrained and impassioned.

> **Go in peace. And may the God of Israel give you what you have asked of him.**
>
> 1 SAMUEL 1:17 MSG

Is there something that you desire with that intensity? What is it that brings tears to your eyes when you think about it for too long?

Let peace permeate your soul—God has received your prayers. If he has promised to fulfill your deepest longing, you can count on the fact that he will. He gave Hannah her child, and he will grant your request as well.

Tonight, take heart that God receives your prayers. Wipe away your tears and receive his peace.

Dear God, thank you so much for receiving my prayers and for drying my tears. I will wait for your answer and fully embrace your peace. Amen.

The LORD gave me what
I asked Him.
1 Samuel 1:27 HCSB

Limitless

God heard the Israelites' cries when they were slaves to Pharaoh in Egypt. He prepared Moses to be their deliverer. He sent ten plagues to convince Pharaoh to set them free. God even parted the Red Sea to help the Israelites escape from the Egyptian army.

> Is the LORD's power limited? Now you shall see whether My word will come true for you.
> NUMBERS 11:23 NASB

After he had done so much for the Israelites, they should have known that his love and power were absolutely limitless—and that he would provide all they needed.

So should you. This evening, be confident that God will do all that he has promised to you. Trust him and be patient. Soon you will see everything he has said come true for you.

Dear God, there is no reason to doubt you. I praise you for your limitless power and love by which you provide for all my needs. Amen.

Yours, O Lord, is the greatness, the power,
the glory, the victory, and the majesty.
Everything in the heavens and on earth is
yours. . . . We adore you as the one
who is over all things.

1 Chronicles 29:11 NLT

Divine Possibilities

God does not ask you to do things that are humanly possible. He does not fill your heart with goals that you could easily achieve on your own.

Rather, God gives you dreams that are far bigger and more wonderful than you could ever aspire to, dreams that can only be accomplished if he is actively involved in your life.

Humanly speaking, it is impossible. But with God everything is possible.
MATTHEW 19:26 NLT

Why? Because God wants you to know that the good that happens to you is from him—so that you will rely upon him.

He is bringing the hopes that burn in you into being. So tonight trust him to make all those impossible dreams come true.

Dear God, with you are divine possibilities. Thank you for letting me join your spectacular plans, and for teaching me to love you more in the process. Amen.

LORD All-Powerful, you are God. You have
promised me some very good things, and you
can be trusted to do what you promise.

2 SAMUEL 7:28 CEV

At School With the Sacred

You cannot avoid problems, but they can be useful to you if you trust God through them. In fact, there is no more profound and effective way to learn spiritual truth than through your troubles.

Your trials train you to rely upon God to overcome your hurdles, and teach you what is really important. They also confirm that he satisfies and nourishes your soul like nothing else can.

> **Though the Lord give you the bread of adversity and the water of affliction, yet . . . your eyes shall see your Teacher.**
> ISAIAH 30:20 ESV

As your instructor, God guides you past many of the pitfalls that lead to or worsen your problems, and he never fails to direct you to his magnificent and enlightening truth.

God truly can make the most of your situation—so fully trust him as your teacher.

Dear God, this evening I thank you for teaching me sacred lessons through this school of my circumstances. I trust you, my beloved teacher. Amen.

My troubles turned out all for the best—they
forced me to learn from your textbook.
Truth from your mouth means more to me
than striking it rich in a gold mine.

PSALM 119:71–72 MSG

God's Kindness

Throughout history, there have been people of great power who have used their influence for selfish, evil purposes. You may even have seen evidence of that today—leaders who wield authority to advance unseemly causes.

> **Because of the mighty power he had used against the Egyptians, the Israelites worshiped him and trusted him and his servant Moses.**
>
> EXODUS 14:31 CEV

God's strength is consistently employed in showing love and freedom to his people. By his power, he freed the Israelites from slavery in Egypt, and they trusted him because of it.

You can trust him too. Though his power is absolutely unlimited, you never need to fear—it is always used for your benefit. The kindness behind God's power will always guard his plans for you and is forever employed in making your way wonderful.

Dear God, thank you for both your kindness and power—for loving me so much that you always do what is best for me. Amen.

You will lead the people You have
redeemed with Your faithful love;
You will guide [them] to Your holy
dwelling with Your strength.

Exodus 15:13 HCSB

You Have All You Need

It is indeed an interesting paradox that the closer you grow to God, the less convinced you become of your own goodness. That is because as your acquaintance with him increases, the more he reveals what you could be—the excellent person he is making you into.

> His divine power has given us everything required for life and godliness, through the knowledge of Him who called us.
>
> 2 PETER 1:3 HCSB

And the greater your feelings of unworthiness at aspiring to his wonderful character, the more he assures you that the seeds of true godliness have taken root in you and are evidenced by your humility.

Part of God's goodness is how he develops you into the very best you can be. So tonight, praise him for providing every tool you need to get there.

Dear God, thank you that even the humility I feel is evidence of growing more in your image. Thank you for making me godly. Amen.

There is something I'm looking for:
a person simple and plain, reverently
responsive to what I say.

Isaiah 66:2 MSG

Seeing God's Good Plan

Joseph's brothers were cruel—they sold him to traveling merchants. They set about a chain of events in Joseph's life that ended with him in a position of prominence, where he could greatly assist people during a challenging time.

> **God sent me on ahead of you to keep your families alive and to save you in this wonderful way.**
> GENESIS 45:7 CEV

Joseph could have been bitter about his difficult life, but he realized that God had worked everything out so that he could help others. And so Joseph forgave his brothers and was also gracious to them.

Tonight, you may be distraught over others' actions. You can be certain, however, that when you see God's plan unfold, you will find he has transformed everything into good and for the blessing of others.

Dear God, help me see the goodness of your plans and forgive those around me. Through my circumstances, make me your instrument for helping others. Amen.

The LORD's plans stand firm forever; his
intentions can never be shaken. What joy
for the nation whose God is the LORD, whose
people he has chosen for his own.

PSALM 33:11–12 NLT

Restored, Confirmed, Strengthened, Established

As you finally settle down this evening, maybe you feel that you are being torn down by your troubles—rather than built up by your God.

> **The God of all grace, who has called you to his eternal glory in Christ, will himself restore, confirm, strengthen, and establish you.**
> 1 PETER 5:10 ESV

Yet both are working together. You see, there are traits within you fighting against the spiritual nature that God is fortifying. At the moment, the pressures you experience are removing them so that God can replace them with qualities that are infinitely better.

Rejoice that God is restoring you with his wisdom, confirming his purpose in your life, strengthening you with heavenly power, and establishing the eternal nature within you.

Dear God, thank you for removing my transitory qualities and replacing them with an everlasting nature. I praise you for restoring, confirming, strengthening, and establishing me. Amen.

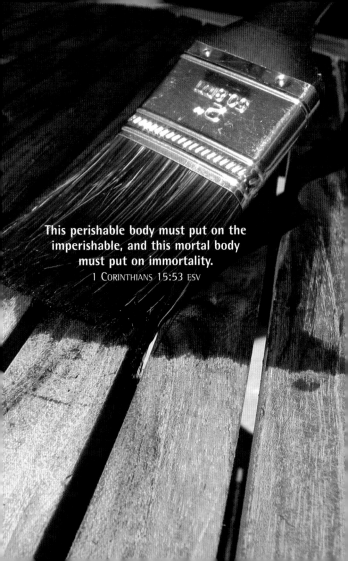

This perishable body must put on the imperishable, and this mortal body must put on immortality.

1 Corinthians 15:53 ESV

He Accepts You

Emotions can become so overwhelming that they drown out all reason. The adrenaline rushes and suddenly unfortunate words flow forcefully.

Have you been there? Have you experienced the flood of remorse—wishing you could retract your words because of how disrespectful they are? Perhaps you even imagined that your tirade damaged your relationship with God.

> When I became embittered and my innermost being was wounded, I was a fool and didn't understand. . . . Yet I am always with You.
>
> PSALM 73:21–23 HCSB

Fear not—God is unmoved. He is still with you and steadfastly accepts you. You see, God knows where your hurt comes from, and his main goal is to heal you. God is strong enough to bear what you say. Approach him with confidence tonight.

Dear God, thank you for loving me when I feel unlovable, and for forgiving my words and healing me. Truly, you are full of grace and mercy. Amen.

Even before there is a
word on my tongue,
behold, O LORD, You
know it all.

PSALM 139:4 NASB

Moments of Peace
for the Evening

Let us hold unswervingly to the hope we profess, for he who promised is faithful.

HEBREWS 10:23 NIV

Unswervingly Faithful

Your challenge this evening is to put aside your doubts. Though circumstances may be disheartening, you must look beyond them to the absolute faithfulness of your God.

Friend, no matter how long you have believed in God, you will have moments of weakness. You will be tempted to believe that it is impossible to surmount what's ahead.

> **Let us hold unswervingly to the hope we profess, for he who promised is faithful.**
>
> Hebrews 10:23 NIV

Your best remedy is to focus on the One who is absolutely true—consistently faithful. God perfectly guides and equips you for the journey—keeping you from swerving away from your purpose.

Cling to him tonight and forget your fears, for the One who promised you would never let you down.

Dear God, thank you for keeping my heart from swerving. I know that even if I cannot see what's ahead, you are faithfully active in my situation. Amen.

We live by faith, not by sight.
2 Corinthians 5:7 NIV

Sustaining Certainty

Does it ever puzzle you how the strength and certainty you received from God yesterday or this morning was only sufficient for a while? That you need to keep going back to God in order to sustain your faith?

> **Study GOD and his strength, seek his presence day and night; remember all the wonders he performed.**
>
> 1 CHRONICLES 16:11–12 MSG

You are not weak. The need to keep going back is actually evidence that your relationship with God is healthy. God has fashioned his encouragement this way because he wants you to return to him. He desires for you to speak with him often and continually draw from his grace.

Go to him tonight—study him, seek his goodness, and remember his power. Sustain your faith, strength, and certainty by staying in the presence of God.

Dear God, I need you. Thank you for always giving me strength and that I can always go to you when I need my faith renewed. Amen.

Praise the Lord, God our Savior,
who helps us every day.
PSALM 68:19 NCV

Know That You're Growing

In the evening hours, when all is quiet, the thought may drift across your mind, *How do I know that Jesus is really having an impact on my life?*

Peter taught that there are certain qualities that indicate that you are growing to be more like Jesus, and you achieve them by praying, studying the Bible, and imitating Jesus' example. Faith, goodness, knowledge, self-control, perseverance, godliness, kindness, and love—all demonstrate that Jesus is actively transforming you.

> If you possess these qualities in increasing measure, they will keep you from being ineffective and unproductive in your knowledge of our Lord Jesus Christ.
>
> 2 PETER 1:8 NIV

Knowing that you are growing is important, so keep adding these qualities to your character. Jesus is shaping you.

Dear God, I do want to be more like Jesus. Please help me to add these qualities through prayer, Bible study, and imitating your example. Amen.

Let the wonderful kindness and the understanding that come from our Lord and Savior Jesus Christ help you to keep on growing. Praise Jesus now and forever!

2 PETER 3:18 CEV

Honoring God's Timing

David was chosen by God to be Israel's second king. The only problem was that Israel's first king, Saul, was still alive.

You may imagine that David got impatient as the years went by and Saul continued to rule. Yet even when he was given the opportunity to kill Saul, he refrained because it was more important for him to honor God than to sit on the throne.

> **I should not do anything against him, because he is the LORD's appointed king!**
> 1 SAMUEL 24:6 NCV

Perhaps you are in a similar situation of waiting. You could do something about it, but you are certain that your remedy would not please God.

Take David's example and honor God's timing tonight. God will certainly bless your patience and self-control.

Dear God, the waiting is so difficult—but I will trust you. I know you are working through this time and doing great things for me. Amen.

With all my heart, I am waiting, Lord, for you! I trust your promises.

Psalm 130:5 CEV

From Doubt to Certainty

Philosopher Sir Francis Bacon once wrote, "If a man begins with certainties, he shall end in doubts; but if he begins with doubts, he shall end in certainties."

As you get to know God, you will have many questions. These are actually beneficial because the search for answers matures your faith. It is far better for you to diligently examine and confirm your beliefs than to accept them at face value.

> I love those who love me, and those who seek me diligently will find me.
> PROVERBS 8:17 NKJV

God encourages you to experience his answers personally. Ask God about the things that perplex you, and look to Scripture for his answers. He will transform your doubts into certainties.

Dear God, thank you for answering my questions and making my faith firm. Thank you for loving me unconditionally and for transforming all of my doubts into certainties. Amen.

May God bless you with
his special favor and
wonderful peace as
you come to know
Jesus, our God and
Lord, better and better.

2 PETER 1:2 NLT

A Motivating Force

Absolutely everything that God does for you is prompted by his love. Though some imagine that God does things out of anger or a desire to control, Scripture is clear that God is motivated by his love for you.

> **Christ's love compels us.**
> 2 CORINTHIANS 5:14
> HCSB

With that in mind, it is clear what should inspire your interaction with God. Though respect is always appropriate, love is the primary impetus for how you respond to him.

Fear, obligation, and selfish ambition should never be the basis of your relationship with God. Serve him gladly out of love because of the love he has shown to you. It is the most wonderful and powerfully motivating force you will ever need.

Dear God, thank you for doing all things out of love—and that love is what you desire in return. May it grow within me exponentially. Amen.

Cheerfully pleasing God is the main thing,
and that's what we aim to do,
regardless of our conditions.

2 CORINTHIANS 5:9 MSG

Rebuilding With Hope

During Israel's arid summer months—when the rivers were dried up—people would build their houses on the sandy shores. Unfortunately, when the rainy season began, the river floodwaters would rise and sweep away their homes.

> **O storm-battered city, troubled and desolate! I will rebuild you on a foundation of sapphires and make the walls of your houses from precious jewels.**
>
> ISAIAH 54:11 NLT

Has this ever happened to you? Have you ever built your hopes on something—a job, relationship, or circumstance—and had all of your security swept away when you lost it?

Thankfully, there is a foundation that stands up to the storms and floods of life. God will not fail you. Rebuild with hope by basing your life on God. He gives you a home that is simply heavenly.

Dear God, thank you for giving me a foundation that is solid—that nothing can wash away. Thank you for rebuilding my life with your marvelous hope. Amen.

Everyone who hears my words and obeys
them is like a wise man who built his house
on rock. It rained hard, the floods came,
and the winds blew and hit that house.
But it did not fall.

MATTHEW 7:24–25 NCV

Thankful Reminiscing

Have you given thanks for your loved ones today? Or have your thoughts been turned to nitpicky grievances and disagreements? Are you dwelling more on what they have done wrong than what they've done to show you love?

> **I give thanks to my God for every remembrance of you, always praying with joy for all of you in my every prayer.**
> PHILIPPIANS 1:3–4
> HCSB

Sometimes it is difficult to redirect your thoughts during a conflict. However, these are the people God has given you to love, and through whom he is perfecting your ability to love him.

Turn your thoughts toward thankfulness this evening by reminiscing over all the good times you have had together. You will find that the great and joyful difference it makes in your relationship will be well worth it.

Dear God, I do give you thanks for my loved ones. Help me to appreciate and enjoy them all the days that we have been given together. Amen.

I know that I am right to think like this about all of you, because I have you in my heart. All of you share in God's grace with me.

PHILIPPIANS 1:7 NCV

The Unseen Dynamic

Were there events today that shook your faith? Were there incidents that made it seem like God was not working in your situation? These will necessarily arise because God is building your faith.

> We do not focus on what is seen, but on what is unseen; for what is seen is temporary, but what is unseen is eternal.
>
> 2 CORINTHIANS 4:18
> HCSB

God is allowing that which is seen as temporary to seemingly contradict what you know to be his purposes for you. Why? Because your faith is built by what is unseen. All evidence may point to defeat, but with God—whose person and work are invisible—is victory.

When circumstances shake your faith, never forget God's unseen workings. Focus on God; believe in him. What you see is temporary, and your triumph is eternal.

Dear God, it is hard to focus on the invisible. Yet I trust you. I praise you for accomplishing great things for me in the unseen. Amen.

Hope that is seen is not hope; for why does one still hope for what he sees? But if we hope for what we do not see, we eagerly wait for it with perseverance.

ROMANS 8:24–25 NKJV

Work for Peaceful Times

In the Old Testament, King Solomon waited until there were no wars or disasters to build God's temple. This was so he could direct all of his attention and resources to it and construct the exceptional building God deserved.

> **God has given me rest on every side. . . . And so I intend to build a house for the name of the LORD.**
> 1 KINGS 5:4–5 ESV

Today, God has a new temple in which to work—you. He gives you times of rest and peace in order to build your relationship with him through prayer, worship, Bible study, and service.

Use peaceful times to build yourself up in the love and knowledge of God. Let him make you into a strong temple so that when challenges come, you will be in excellent spiritual shape to face them.

Dear God, thank you for giving me such meaningful work for times of peace. Help me to be a wonderful temple for you to work through. Amen.

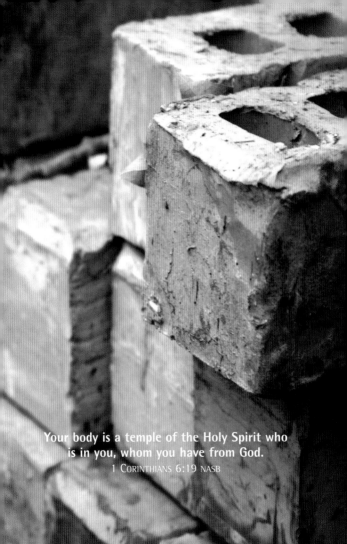

Your body is a temple of the Holy Spirit who
is in you, whom you have from God.

1 CORINTHIANS 6:19 NASB

On the Path to the Promise

The question is not whether God will do as he promised—he absolutely will. Rather, it is whether you will believe him and persevere until you reach the goal.

> **Patient endurance is what you need now, so you will continue to do God's will. Then you will receive all that he has promised.**
> HEBREWS 10:36 NLT

You are on the path to the promise. Though the landscape looks nothing like your destination, God is expertly navigating your course. Steep mountains may block your way, and though you cannot go over or around—he leads you through them.

If you follow God faithfully, you will find that the promise far surpasses your greatest hopes.

Tonight, patiently persevere to do God's will because the reward is truly astounding.

Dear God, sometimes waiting is extremely difficult. However, I will trust you every step on the path to the promise because I know you are faithful. Amen.

Do not, therefore, fling away your fearless
confidence, for it carries a great and
glorious compensation of reward.

HEBREWS 10:35 AMP

He Always Hears You

Oh the great and wonderful joy of knowing that you have been heard. He is the God whose ear is ever attentive to you. He listens closely for your call, as a caring mother listens for the cry of her newborn baby.

> I waited patiently for the LORD, and He turned to me and heard my cry for help.
>
> PSALM 40:1 HCSB

With his powerful hand he helps you. With his profound love he comforts you. He just wants to hear your voice calling to him. He merely wants you to trust him enough to seek him.

Tonight beckon him, and he will help you. Ask and he shall provide for your deepest needs. Patiently watch for him, and you will see all his glorious resources employed in answering you.

Dear God, thank you for listening to me. Truly, you are great and mighty—abounding in love for those who trust in you. Amen.

Keep on asking, and you will be given
what you ask for. Keep on looking,
and you will find. Keep on knocking,
and the door will be opened.

LUKE 11:9 NLT

Pillars of Provision

When Moses led the Israelites out of Egypt, slavery was all they understood. They didn't know the land, the challenges ahead, or even how to defend themselves. So God gave them the pillars of cloud and fire as visual reminders of his presence, protection, and guidance.

> **The LORD went before them by day in a pillar of cloud to lead the way, and by night in a pillar of fire to give them light.**
> EXODUS 13:21 NKJV

When God leads you into areas you are not acquainted with, he gives you pillars of provision as well. They may be Bible verses, songs, or even godly friends who turn up whenever you need a reminder that you are not alone.

When you receive those pillars, praise God. He is assuring you of his presence—and guiding and protecting every step of your journey.

Dear God, I praise you for lighting my way and protecting me. Thank you for the powerful reminders that you are always with me. Amen.

I will guide them on paths they have not
known. I will turn darkness to light in
front of them, and rough places into level
ground. . . . I will not forsake them.

ISAIAH 42:16 HCSB

His Answer to You

It is sad when people refuse to seek God out of fear that he will reject their weaknesses and expect them to be perfect. They do not realize that God loves them unconditionally.

In fact, Scripture teaches that God is repeatedly moved by compassion and gladly serves those who need him. He never turns away those who earnestly seek him; he embraces them and cares for them deeply.

> **Moved with compassion, Jesus stretched out His hand and touched him, and said to him, "I am willing; be cleansed."**
> MARK 1:41 NASB

Your problems cannot disqualify you from receiving God's love. When you ask, he *always* answers that he is willing to heal your hurts.

Seek God with confidence. He is kind and compassionate, and is glad when you trust him enough to call.

Dear God, thank you for always being willing to help me. You are truly loving and merciful. May I never stop seeking you. Amen.

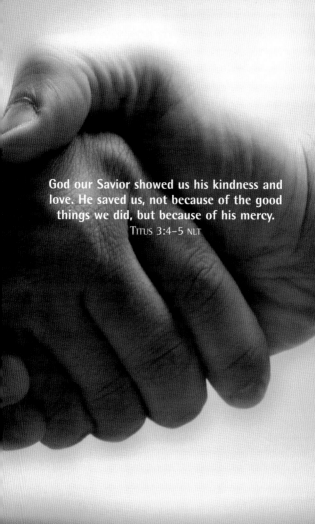

God our Savior showed us his kindness and love. He saved us, not because of the good things we did, but because of his mercy.

TITUS 3:4–5 NLT

Moments of Peace
for the Evening

We know that God causes everything
to work together for the good
of those who love God.

ROMANS 8:28 NLT

Your Best for the Next Generation

What is your legacy? What do you leave behind? Do your loved ones look forward to the things they will inherit? Or do they aspire to following your example?

> **Please let there be a double portion of your spirit on me.**
> 2 KINGS 2:9 ESV

There is a story in Scripture about a great prophet named Elijah, who granted his apprentice a request before he was taken up to God. The apprentice was so inspired by knowing Elijah that he asked for a double portion of Elijah's amazing spirit.

Similarly, the most meaningful thing you can leave for the next generation is your example of love and dedication to God.

Is that how you are living? Will others want a double portion of your spirit?

Dear God, I've thought about providing for my family financially—but a spiritual legacy is even more important. May my spirit truly inspire them to follow you. Amen.

These are things we learned from our ancestors, and we will tell them to the next generation. We won't keep secret the glorious deeds and the mighty miracles of the Lord.

PSALM 78:3–4 CEV

Each and Every Thing

Not everything that comes into your life will be good, but God can use it for good. Not all events will fit into your understanding. However, he has the understanding to make each incident fit into his plan.

> **We know that God causes everything to work together for the good of those who love God.**
> ROMANS 8:28 NLT

God works through everything that happens to you. He does not allow one experience to go to waste.

Tonight, you may not be able to explain why something has occurred in your life. Yet you can be confident that God is wise enough to transform it into something for his purpose.

Because of his great mercy, someday you will look back and see the good he has accomplished through it.

Dear God, thank you for the assurance that you cause everything to work for good. It gives me the hope and confidence to go on. Amen.

Trust in God at all times, my people. Tell
him all your troubles, for he is our refuge.

PSALM 62:8 GNT

Receive His Strength

Isn't it amazing that God wants to prove himself to you? He knows there will be situations that you are not strong enough to handle, and he wants you to fully trust in him as your defender.

> **The eyes of the LORD range throughout the earth to show Himself strong for those whose hearts are completely His.**
> 2 CHRONICLES 16:9
> HCSB

Has some recent incident exposed an area of your weakness? Are you discouraged because it goes to the heart of who you want to be? Be encouraged that it is a phenomenal opportunity for God to show you his power.

Give your heart to him completely tonight, and receive his strength. Not only will you have all the power you need, but you will also have proof of God's faithfulness.

Dear God, you know my weaknesses. Please show yourself strong on my behalf. I praise you for teaching me to trust in your strength. Amen.

O Lord GOD, you have only begun to show
your servant your greatness and your mighty
hand. For what god is there in heaven or on
earth who can do such works and
mighty acts as yours?

DEUTERONOMY 3:24 ESV

An Able Protector

The time had come for the Israelites to conquer the expansive land they had been promised. It must have been daunting for them to face such an amazing challenge. They understood, however, that their future was safely in God's hands and that he would never let them down.

> **Do not be afraid of them! The LORD your God will go ahead of you. He will neither fail you nor forsake you.**
>
> DEUTERONOMY 31:6 NLT

Has your rest been disturbed by thoughts of tomorrow? Are you daunted by the situation you will face? Take courage tonight that God leads you. As he did with the Israelites, he prepares the way for your triumph.

He is able to protect you and will never fail. Rest easy that tomorrow is completely in his hands.

Dear God, I praise you for leading the way. Thank you for calming my fears and preparing the way of victory for me. Amen.

You won't have to lift a hand in this battle;
just stand firm . . . and watch God's saving
work for you take shape. Don't be afraid,
don't waver. March out boldly
tomorrow—God is with you.

2 CHRONICLES 20:17 MSG

Good Investments

This evening, are you frustrated with the small scope of your lot? Do you wish for opportunities of greater influence, responsibility, and reward?

Your present situation may be limited. God, however, has given it as an investment in your future. Were you to have all the success you desire, you may have found yourself ill equipped to handle it. Worse, you might have missed the greatest gift of all—a fulfilling relationship with God.

> **He who is faithful in what is least is faithful also in much.**
> LUKE 16:10 NKJV

In your current circumstances, God is able to teach you what is truly valuable and build the character necessary for success. Therefore, faithfully invest yourself in whatever God gives you and soon he will trust with even greater opportunities.

Dear God, please help me to be faithful with little so that you can eventually trust me with more. Thank you for investing in my success. Amen.

Well done, good
and faithful
servant; you have
been faithful over
a few things, I will
make you ruler
over many things.
Enter into the joy
of your lord.

MATTHEW 25:23 NKJV

A Right Attitude

When you receive new information—facts that show you have been heading in the wrong direction or have made a faulty decision—there are two basic tracks you can choose. You can either malign the new details or admit that you have been misinformed.

> You were sorry and humbled yourself before the LORD when you heard what I said . . . so I have indeed heard you, says the LORD.
> 2 KINGS 22:19 NLT

Though the mistake may not have been your fault, God is pleased when your heart is responsive. When you show humility, you communicate that you desire excellence in your work and that you are willing to make things right.

When you have the right attitude, God honors you. So be humble, and be blessed by how delightfully God defends you.

Dear God, thank you for helping me when I make wrong decisions. Help me to be humble so that I may always please you. Amen.

Humble yourselves before the Lord,
and He will exalt you.

JAMES 4:10 HCSB

A New Hometown

Whatever you achieve here on earth—whether it results in lofty prestige or lowly anonymity—you have a great reward awaiting you. It is your final destination, a city of light and happiness, where God is praised and every tear is wiped away.

> **The city did not need the sun or the moon. The glory of God was shining on it, and the Lamb was its light.**
> REVELATION 21:23 CEV

When you believe in God, you know for certain that heaven will be your everlasting hometown. All of the pain and injustice you've experienced will fade from your memory. You will be filled with joy because God will light your life.

Therefore, thank God tonight that no matter what happens here on earth, he has provided a place for you in heaven. Truly, there is no place like *that* home.

Dear God, I praise you that through your amazing provision I have a remarkable new hometown. Thank you for such a sustaining and spectacular hope. Amen.

In my Father's house are many rooms. If it were not so, would I have told you that I go to prepare a place for you?

JOHN 14:2 ESV

Effective Defenses

In ancient times, a city's strength was found in the walls that surrounded it—its defense against marauders and attacking armies.

> **A person without self-control is as defenseless as a city with broken-down walls.**
> PROVERBS 25:28 NLT

Today, depending on where you live, you probably have features that keep your home safe, such as locks on your doors or a security system. Though those devices limit your movement, they protect you from harm.

So it is when you practice self-control. Whether you guard your health by eating well and keeping fit, or protect your finances by spending and investing wisely, discipline is your effective defense to a life well lived.

You are strengthened by self-control. Exercise discipline in every area of your life.

Dear God, self-control is not easy, but it is definitely good. Please help me to be disciplined and to follow your excellent, life-preserving statutes.
Amen.

If you want to live securely in the land, keep my laws and obey my regulations. Then the land will yield bumper crops, and you will eat your fill and live securely in it.

LEVITICUS 25:18–19 NLT

Sincere Motivation

This evening, contemplate this: Why do you love those who are dearest to you?

Is it because of their physical beauty or strength? Or because they have loved you—treating you with particularly tender kindness? Perhaps they have made extraordinary sacrifices on your behalf?

> **Love one another fervently with a pure heart.**
>
> 1 PETER 1:22 NKJV

Though all of these issues may factor in, your true inspiration originates from one source—God's love for you.

It is through the overflow of God's unconditional love that you are sincerely motivated to love another—even if they offer nothing in return. And so, when beauty and strength fade and sacrifices are forgotten, your love remains strong and steadfast because that is what God has done for you.

Dear God, thank you for loving me. Please help to love others unconditionally as you would. When all else fails, your love endures. Amen.

We love, because He first loved us.

1 JOHN 4:19 NASB

As He Loved You

Human love is generally described as a feeling and is often based on fleeting passions. Outwardly, even minor things can affect its disposition, because it looks inward—to its own interests. And it grows harder and less trusting with each experience.

> **Beloved, if God loved us so [very much], we also ought to love one another.**
>
> 1 JOHN 4:11 AMP

However, God's love is different from human love. His love is not an emotion; rather, it is a deliberate, consistent action that is given unconditionally. His love is not moved by circumstances because it looks outward—to your best interest.

Therefore, love others with God's kind of love this evening. No doubt others will respond well to his unconditional love and will find *you* absolutely lovely.

Dear God, teach me to love as you do—to be deliberate, unconditional, tender, and outwardly focused. Help me to always seek the good of the other person. Amen.

Dear friends, let us love one another,
because love comes from God. Whoever
loves is a child of God and knows God.

1 JOHN 4:7 GNT

Celebration and Praise

Expressing praise to God can take many forms. Scripture teaches that David danced before him. Yet David also wrote worshipful psalms to express his appreciation. Some have sung hymns to thank God for his goodness, while others have played their musical instruments.

> **David danced before the Lord with all his might.**
> 2 SAMUEL 6:14 AMP

How do you praise God? Do you lift your hands in exaltation? Or do you drop to your knees in humble adoration? Is a tambourine your instrument for rejoicing? Or do you express your passion through poems?

Whatever it is, the important thing is that you are celebrating God. This evening, whether you dance or paint, sing or are silent—make sure you give your wonderful God all of the glory.

Dear God, thank you for accepting my unique expression of praise. I exalt you with all of my heart, my beloved God. Amen.

Praise him with castanets and dance, praise him with banjo and flute. . . . Let every living, breathing creature praise GOD! Hallelujah!

PSALM 150:4, 6 MSG

Famine or Feast?

Bitterness is a draining emotion that compounds feelings of emptiness and defeat. It stems from unforgiveness and can make you feel isolated. Like eating air, the more of it you consume, the more starved and unfulfilled you feel.

> **He who is of a merry heart has a continual feast.**
> PROVERBS 15:15 NKJV

Yet you do not have to accept that emptiness. You can feed your heart joy and forgiveness by remembering God's faithfulness and grace to you. Instead of being drained and isolated, you can be filled and satisfied with his love.

Do you desire a joyful heart this evening? God wants to fill you. However, you must release your bitterness and forgive those who hurt you. So do it. Your heart will certainly benefit from your change in diet.

Dear God, please help me to let go of my bitterness and forgive others. Thank you so much for satisfying my heart and filling me with your joy. Amen.

Your love, GOD, took hold and held me fast.
When I was upset and beside myself, you
calmed me down and cheered me up.

PSALM 94:18–19 MSG

Only Believe

Jairus had nowhere else to go. His little girl was dying, and the others in his household had given up hope that she would recover. So Jairus went to Jesus.

You may be in the same kind of dilemma—a situation so difficult that everyone else gives up. It may look hopeless; however, God says the same to you as Jesus said to Jairus. "Don't be afraid. Just believe."

Do not be afraid; only believe.
MARK 5:36 NKJV

Jesus healed Jairus's daughter. God can do wondrous things in your situation too. You don't ever have to lose hope as long as you believe in him. You just have to trust him.

Dear God, I do trust you. Thank you that you are with me in my situation and I don't need to be afraid. Amen.

Don't panic. I'm with you. There's no need to fear for I'm your God. I'll give you strength. I'll help you. I'll hold you steady, keep a firm grip on you.

ISAIAH 41:10 MSG

Bound by Peace

There is but one way to be unified—though it is not through uniformity. When people are forced to conform, their God-given differences are often squelched. Rather, the way to unity is for each person to be obedient to the Lord.

> **Always keep yourselves united in the Holy Spirit, and bind yourselves together with peace.**
> EPHESIANS 4:3 NLT

God would never contradict himself, so when everyone is doing as he says, they are actually working toward the same goal—whether they realize it or not.

The wonderful product of everyone doing his or her unique part—focusing on him rather than on the work or each other—is peace. To be united in him is to be bound by peace—the best and most effective way to get anything done.

Dear God, I pray we would all be devoted to serving you wholeheartedly so that we would have the peace and unity that glorify you. Amen.

You were all called to travel on the same
road and in the same direction, so stay
together, both outwardly and inwardly. . . .
Everything you are and think and do is
permeated with Oneness.

EPHESIANS 4:4, 6 MSG

Moments of Peace
for the Evening

I will tell of the LORD's
unfailing love. I will praise
the LORD for all he has done.
I will rejoice in his great
goodness.
ISAIAH 63:7 NLT

With Spirit and With Sword

When the Israelites rebuilt the temple after the Babylonian captivity, they continued to be surrounded by dangerous enemies. They protected themselves with spirit-led prayers and guards with swords.

Their combination of spirit and sword illustrates a valuable lesson of faith. The first is to trust God's power through prayer, knowing he will provide for you and protect you. The second part involves obedience to God with your earthly resources. You do as he instructs, and he gives you the ability to carry it out.

> **We countered with prayer to our God and set a round-the-clock guard against them.**
> NEHEMIAH 4:9 MSG

So then, whatever obstacles you face tonight, overcome them with spirit and sword—with trust in God and obedience to him. That combination is a winner.

Dear God, every battle requires that you and I do our parts. I will trust your provision and guidance, and you will lead the way to victory. Amen.

I obey you with all my heart, and I trust you,
knowing that you will save me.

PSALM 25:21 CEV

Avoiding the Paralysis
of Analysis

No race has ever been won or great work achieved by looking back. In order to live effectively, you must realize that your victories and defeats are only brushstrokes in the larger picture of your life. Your purpose can only be fully realized if you diligently carry on painting after them.

> I am focusing all my energies on this one thing: Forgetting the past and looking forward to what lies ahead.
>
> PHILIPPIANS 3:13 NLT

True, there is worth in evaluating your experiences. They should teach you pitfalls to avoid and flaws to fix. However, there comes a point when analyzing your past paralyzes you, when it defines your brushstrokes and stops you from being creative.

This evening, look ahead by focusing on God. Courageously continue on. With God's help, your life will be a beautiful work of art.

Dear God, help me to release the past and keep my eye on where you want me to go. Thank you for having wonderful plans for my life. Amen.

Always honor the Lord. Then you will truly have hope for the future.
PROVERBS 23:17–18 CEV

Flourishing in the Difficult Places

Do you ever feel utterly squeezed of every resource? As if—like an over-tilled field—you were completely emptied of creativity? Yet circumstances make it necessary for you to keep going. What can you do?

> **The LORD will guide you always; he will satisfy your needs in a sun-scorched land. . . . You will be like a well-watered garden.**
>
> ISAIAH 58:11 NIV

It is during those times that your only choice is to turn to God—and he does a marvelous work in you. In those difficult places, God wondrously makes you flourish.

Tonight, you may have come to the end of your fruitfulness—but you also have come to the beginning of God's. He will miraculously turn your toil-scorched spirit into a well-watered garden of inspiration. Your finest ideas bloom when he is doing the gardening.

Dear God, I praise you for making things grow in barren places. Fill me with your spirit so that I may glorify you with excellent work. Amen.

Those who are planted in the house of the Lord shall flourish in the courts of our God.

PSALM 92:13 NKJV

Worthy of Repeating

How often do you remember God's goodness? Surely he has accomplished great things for you. Even now, he brings to mind the many times when he has shown you his love.

> **I will tell of the LORD's unfailing love. I will praise the LORD for all he has done. I will rejoice in his great goodness.**
>
> ISAIAH 63:7 NLT

There is an amazing benefit to meditating on all God has done. Dwell on his goodness and it will inspire you. Recall his excellent works and your faith will be renewed. Express your appreciation for his provision and your trust in his flawless character—and your heart will soar to the threshold of heaven.

Nothing encourages your soul or pleases God like praise. So exalt him for all the joy he has given you. His glorious acts are certainly worth repeating.

Dear God, how can I thank you enough for your love to me? I praise you for your astounding faithfulness and dazzling works. Amen.

O Lord, You are my God; I will exalt You, I
will give thanks to Your name; for You have
worked wonders, plans formed long ago,
with perfect faithfulness.

Isaiah 25:1 NASB

There is a purpose for your life. Perhaps you know of some ways you need to straighten your course, but God has excellent plans for you and will guide you if you are willing. He knew what you would need before he even began putting you together.

Before I shaped you in the womb, I knew all about you. Before you saw the light of day, I had holy plans for you.
JEREMIAH 1:5 MSG

If there is some challenge ahead that you feel inadequate to face, do not fear. God knows what you can handle and he knows what he must teach you in order for you to succeed.

Tonight, thank him for his deep knowledge and wonderful purpose for you. Sleep well knowing that he has equipped you with everything you need for the future.

Dear God, thank you so much for the fantastic plans you have for my life—and for empowering me to succeed in them. Truly, you are wonderful. Amen.

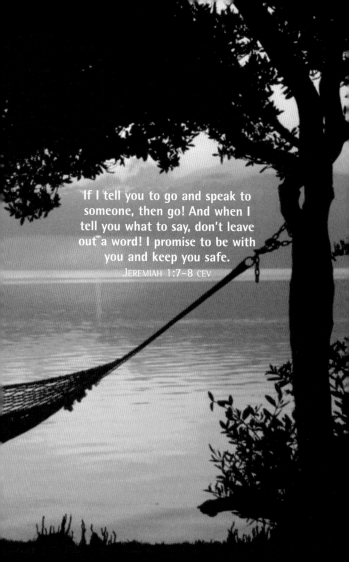

If I tell you to go and speak to someone, then go! And when I tell you what to say, don't leave out a word! I promise to be with you and keep you safe.

JEREMIAH 1:7–8 CEV

Peter and Andrew spent their days casting nets into the Sea of Galilee. Undoubtedly, it was for feeding their families and others.

Providing for needs is a noble enough purpose—yet when Jesus called them to become fishers of men, he was asking them to aspire to more.

> **Come after Me [as disciples— letting Me be your Guide], follow Me, and I will make you fishers of men!**
> MATTHEW 4:19 AMP

Certainly there are many excellent pursuits on which to spend one's life. Imagine being the conduit through which God changes a life. Not just feeding a person's stomach but the person's heart. Not just healing a person's body but the person's soul.

God appeals to your desire to help others by giving you an amazing purpose—influencing a person's view of eternity.

Dear God, you fill my life with an astounding purpose—to introduce people to you. Help me to follow you and inspire others to do so as well. Amen.

When you heard his message from us, you accepted it as the word of God, not the words of humans. And it really is God's message which works in you who believe.

1 THESSALONIANS 2:13 NCV

Representing His Presence

Whether you realize it or not, you shape how others see God. If a person meets Christians who are anxious, harsh, and bitter, he or she will assume that God must be the same way.

> **Let your gentle spirit be known to all men. The Lord is near.**
> PHILIPPIANS 4:5 NASB

If the believer exudes a rejoicing heart, a gentle spirit, and a trusting attitude no matter what happens, the person will know that something supernatural is at work. He or she will see the love and kindness of God lived out in the flesh.

God works through you to show others he is real and very near. Are you representing him well today? Your good example may encourage someone to experience his presence in a deeper way.

Dear God, when others meet me, I want them to know how loving and real you are in my life. Please teach me to represent you well. Amen.

Let us hold true to what we have already attained and walk and order our lives by that. Brethren, together follow my example and observe those who live after the pattern we have set for you.

PHILIPPIANS 3:16–17 AMP

Your Majestic Leader

Of all the great rulers, none has ever compared to God. No sovereign has ever been so magnificently majestic or profoundly wise. No leader has ever been so good to his people—or has provided such an opulent and wonderful future for them.

> **On his robe and thigh was written this title: King of kings and Lord of lords.**
>
> REVELATION 19:16
> NLT

Some may inspire, yet none to his heights. Others may gain glory, but are dim in comparison to his brilliant splendor.

Tonight, praise the monarch of heaven, the greatest king of all. Praise the almighty God—the Lord above all others—who wins every battle and whose kingdom has no end.

Trust him who is enthroned above, for he leads you out of love and does all his greatest works on your behalf.

Dear God, you are my God and King—and I praise you. You are the excellent ruler of heaven and earth. Blessed be your name. Amen.

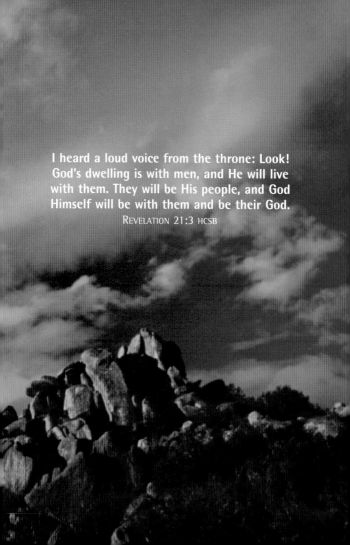

I heard a loud voice from the throne: Look! God's dwelling is with men, and He will live with them. They will be His people, and God Himself will be with them and be their God.

REVELATION 21:3 HCSB

Remembering Your Work and Love

It has been said that it is easier for people to believe negative facts than positive ones—to remember the wrong that has been done rather than the good.

However, that is absolutely not true with God. When you believe in him, he promises to absolutely erase any instance when you have fallen short. And he remembers and celebrates all the good works you have done out of love.

> **God is not unjust so as to forget your work and the love which you have shown toward His name.**
> HEBREWS 6:10 NASB

Do you feel at times as if God has forgotten you? God has neither forgotten you nor the ways you have served him. So tonight, rejoice that the thoughts he has toward you are—and will always be—outstanding.

Dear God, thank you so much for your superb thoughts toward me. You do so much for me—thank you for remembering what I have done for you. Amen.

If anyone gives even a cup of cold water
to one of these little ones because he is
my disciple, I tell you the truth, he will
certainly not lose his reward.

MATTHEW 10:42 NIV

Unending Provision

There was a time in Israel when the rains stopped flowing for three years. Because of that, there was no wheat in the fields to make flour or olives to make oil.

It was a very difficult time for everyone—particularly for one widow who was especially committed to serving God. Yet God made sure that she and her son had enough to eat because they did all he asked.

God always provides for those who love and do as he says. So tonight, do not fear lean days. Rather, rejoice that his provision never ends. Obey him, and you will be amazed at how he keeps the flour and oil flowing.

> **Your jar of flour won't run out and your bottle of oil won't dry up before he sends rain for the crops.**
>
> 1 KINGS 17:14 CEV

Dear God, thank you for knowing my needs and constantly providing for me. I will obey you, knowing that you are always faithful to help me. Amen.

I have never seen good people abandoned by the LORD or their children begging for food. At all times they give freely and lend to others, and their children are a blessing.

PSALM 37:25–26 GNT

Worthy of Your Trust

God always prepares your victory—giving you a vision of what he will do, but not of the way to get there. He does this so that you will walk with him daily and trust him for instructions.

> **The One who called you is completely dependable. If he said it, he'll do it!**
> 1 THESSALONIANS 5:24 MSG

However, when you attempt to reach the vision on your own, the journey will always overwhelm you. It is only when you stay close to God that you see his amazing plan unfold in a manner that increases your faith.

God teaches you to trust him one step at a time. Therefore, thank him tonight for the directions he has given you, and praise him for being trustworthy to take you to the vision.

Dear God, you are certainly worthy to lead me. I praise you that, though I cannot see the way ahead, you have already won the victory. Amen.

You have done good things for your
servant, as you have promised, LORD.
Teach me wisdom and knowledge
because I trust your commands.

PSALM 119:65–66 NCV

Knowing He Loves You

The moment you believed in God, all of his goodness and grace were given to you. In a sense, you were clothed with them—as if a spiritual garment covered you.

All of the joy, power, and approval—all the cherished characteristics associated with God—were conferred upon you.

This may be difficult to grasp if you have been reminded of failings or have not previously viewed yourself in such a positive light. However, this is not about you—but about the effect God has on you.

> **I take delight in You!**
> MARK 1:11 HCSB

Be encouraged tonight—no one can take away what God has given to you. His complete love and approval are yours forever, so rejoice and delight yourself in him.

Dear God, I praise you for the wonderful effect you have on me. Thank you for this delightful love and approval that I can never lose. Amen.

God has been so kind to us, and he has accepted us because of Jesus.

ROMANS 5:17 CEV

Showing God You Love Him

Address God with thanksgiving and gladness, for he truly loves to hear your voice. Though he is powerfully involved with all the workings of the world, he is most joyfully rewarded when you tell him you appreciate him.

> **I worship at your holy temple and praise you for your love and your faithfulness. You were true to your word.**
>
> PSALM 138:2 CEV

He is intimately concerned for you—answering when you call, giving you courage for the journey, and teaching you the way to victory. Though you experience troubles, he helps you. Though dangers may come, he protects you. And nothing ever keeps him from fulfilling his promises to you.

Lift your voice tonight, and exalt your God. Praise him, and tell how much you love him. For his heart rejoices with your songs. And, after all, he deserves it.

Dear God, you really do deserve my thanksgiving and praise. You are worthy of honor and glory. May your name be lifted high forever. Amen.

I will sing of your love and justice; to you,
O Lord, I will sing praise.

Psalm 101:1 niv

No Mess-Up Too Big

When English naturalist John Ray wrote "Misery loves company," he tapped on an inherent human characteristic. People relate to those who have similar failings.

If you have ever doubted, you are certainly not alone. After walking with Jesus for three years, Peter denied Jesus in a way that broke his heart. Peter doubted and abandoned Jesus when Jesus needed him most.

> Peter remembered what Jesus had said: "Before the rooster crows, you will deny me three times." He went out and cried and cried and cried.
>
> MATTHEW 26:75 MSG

Yet Jesus powerfully forgave Peter's denial— Peter's biggest mess-up. And Peter went on to be one of Jesus' most wholehearted and effective proponents.

If you relate to Peter's failings tonight, take heart in his findings. God forgives your mistakes as well. Trust him and believe.

Dear God, sometimes I relate to Peter's doubts. Thank you for forgiving me. I know he found you faithful and that I certainly will too. Amen.

My purpose in writing is to encourage you and assure you that the grace of God is with you no matter what happens.

1 PETER 5:12 NLT

Moments of Peace for the Evening

I am the light of the world. He who
follows Me shall not walk in darkness,
but have the light of life.

JOHN 8:12 NKJV

Food for the Mind

The mind is so much like the body—what you put in it makes a difference in how it works. If you eat a lot of junk food, your health deteriorates. Similarly, if you put negative things into your mind, it acts like poison, killing your ability to have faith or live a life that is pleasing to God.

> **You'll do best by filling your minds and meditating on things true, noble, reputable, authentic, compelling, gracious.**
> PHILIPPIANS 4:8 MSG

Paul's admonishment to the Philippians is for you as well: fill your mind with things that are true, noble, reputable, authentic, compelling, and gracious. Such things affect your outlook and empower you to be the best that you can be.

Tonight, feed your mind with thoughts of God and the Bible. His nourishment will never leave you hungry.

Dear God, fill my thoughts with faith. Feed my mind with excellent, worthy thoughts of you so that my life will always be pleasing to you. Amen.

Let God transform you into a new person by changing the way you think. Then you will know what God wants you to do, and you will know how good and pleasing and perfect his will really is.

ROMANS 12:2 NLT

An Ever-Present Defender

Remember who you are: you are God's cherished loved one. You are fully accepted and completely cared for. Keep in mind the privilege bestowed on you. You are given an instant audience whenever you call upon the throne of heaven.

What great nation is there that has a god so near to it as is the LORD our God whenever we call on Him?

DEUTERONOMY 4:7
NASB

It is important that you keep these great gifts in mind so that you do not lose heart or feel alone. Your mighty God is close to you and is always securing your way and constantly available to you.

This evening, allow that truth to fill you with joy. Ask God to reveal his presence to you and to help you understand how awesome he really is. And never, ever forget that he is there.

Dear God, there is never a reason for me to be lonely or afraid, because you are my great and present defender. Thank you. Amen.

You are my hiding place; you shall preserve
me from trouble; you shall surround me with
songs of deliverance.

PSALM 32:7 NKJV

Confident of Light
in Dark Times

Nothing brings darkness to the heart like a lack of vision for the future. Looking forward to tomorrow and seeing nothing certain can be unsettling.

> **I am the light of the world. He who follows Me shall not walk in darkness, but have the light of life.**
> JOHN 8:12 NKJV

Yet you follow Jesus, who not only guides your path but is also the light of it. He knows what is coming and how to prepare you for it. He also promises to be your unwavering hope and joy in it.

Although you have no knowledge of what is ahead, you have faith in the One who goes before you and are confident that he will guide you well.

Do not fear what tomorrow brings. Jesus will be your light. And no darkness will ever separate you from him.

Dear God, I don't know what the future holds, but because of you I have great hope. Thank you for bringing light to my life. Amen.

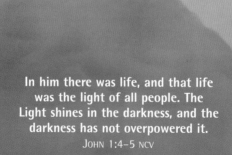

In him there was life, and that life
was the light of all people. The
Light shines in the darkness, and the
darkness has not overpowered it.

JOHN 1:4–5 NCV

Transcending Tranquility

God's peace is an astounding calmness of soul that comes even though all around is confusion. There is no earthly explanation for it. It is simply the tranquility that results from constant communion with God—the assurance that he will thoroughly tame the chaos and bring order to it.

This peace is beyond your comprehension—and it is better than understanding why something is happening to you. You know that if God has allowed these troubles, he will help you through them.

> **With thanksgiving, let your requests be made known to God. And the peace of God, which surpasses every thought, will guard your hearts.**
> PHILIPPIANS 4:6–7
> HCSB

Feel peace in the midst of the commotion. The fact that you are not worrying is evidence that God is doing a transcending work.

Dear God, it is amazing that through all of this you keep my heart calm. I praise you for this peace that is better than understanding. Amen.

In peace I will both lie down and sleep,
for You, Lord, alone make me dwell in
safety and confident trust.

PSALM 4:8 AMP

Readied for Blessings

God's plans are exceedingly strategic and effective. He not only readies good things to fill your life with joy, but he also prepares you with the ability to truly appreciate them.

> **Therefore the LORD will wait, that He may be gracious to you; and therefore He will be exalted, that He may have mercy on you.**
> ISAIAH 30:18 NKJV

There is never regret when God blesses you. There is no looking back and thinking, *If only I had more knowledge, maturity, or skill.* Rather, your exclamation will be about how amazing that God coordinated all factors to culminate in a joyful way.

Be patient this evening. God is strategically ordering good things to bring you great happiness. You will be thrilled when you finally possess the merciful and gracious blessings he has planned for you.

Dear God, I am so eager for your blessings, and yet I know your timing is perfect. Thank you for coordinating everything for the fullness of my joy. Amen.

Out of the fullness of his grace he
has blessed us all, giving us one
blessing after another.

JOHN 1:16 GNT

An Encouraging Word

The stories in the Bible are a gift to help you in times of difficulty. The people in Scripture had challenges and doubts just like you. And God never failed them. Likewise, you know he will always come through for you.

Whatever instructions, promises, and comforts God gave to Abraham, Moses, David, and Paul, he gives to you. Claim them as your own treasures and rejoice in them.

God will make your story into an encouragement as well—helping others to know that they are not alone. Others will be heartened by how God has strengthened you through the Bible.

> **Whatever was written before was written for our instruction, so that through our endurance and through the encouragement of the Scriptures we may have hope.**
> ROMANS 15:4 HCSB

Dear God, thank you for speaking to me so powerfully and for sustaining me through your word. Make my life an inspiring story of faith as well. Amen.

All Scripture is God-breathed and is useful for teaching, rebuking, correcting and training in righteousness, so that the man of God may be thoroughly equipped for every good work.

2 TIMOTHY 3:16–17 NIV

The Unshakable Assurance

The transitory things can be shaken, and it is the temporary nature in you that generates your fears. Worries concerning the future and your legacy can make your soul quiver.

> **Though the mountains move and the hills shake, my love will not be removed from you and My covenant of peace will not be shaken.**
> ISAIAH 54:10 HCSB

God's eternal nature has been given to you as well. Through it you know that your future is eternally secure, and that your heritage is forever tied to the most glorious victory of all—the triumph that provides you with a home in heaven.

God's kindness to you is that he patiently removes all the fleeting things that cause you to fear. The only thing left to make you tremble is your love for him.

Dear God, this evening I thank you for building the unshakable nature in me with the assurance of an eternally secure future and triumphant legacy. Amen.

Let us be thankful, then, because we receive a kingdom that cannot be shaken. Let us be grateful and worship God in a way that will please him, with reverence and awe.

HEBREWS 12:28 GNT

Only the Best

There are those who are afraid to pray to God because they do not feel that they are sufficiently artful to win his approval. They fear saying something wrong or asking for something that would displease him.

> **Which one of you, if his son asks him for bread, will give him a stone?**
> MATTHEW 7:9 ESV

God delights in hearing your prayers. He tenderly contemplates the desires of your heart and thoughtfully arranges for how they are fulfilled. Though he never grants the requests that ultimately cause you harm, he gladly provides what is absolutely best for you.

Tonight, trust God and pray to him. You do not have to be eloquent—you simply need to be sincere. Then accept how he responds as his very best on your behalf.

Dear God, thank you for hearing my prayers. Whether your answer is yes, no, or wait, I know you are providing the very finest for me. Amen.

How much more will your Father
who is in heaven give good
things to those who ask Him!
MATTHEW 7:11 NKJV

Mightily Blessed

Spending time with God will always change you for the better. When you experience his presence, it builds lasting qualities in you like nothing else can. You learn to love the One with whom you will spend eternity and discover how to watch for him.

> What a stack of blessing you have piled up for those who worship you, ready and waiting for all who run to you.
>
> PSALM 31:19 MSG

Surely, there are an abundance of earthly blessings for you—good things that God gives you to encourage your heart. At the same time, he is awakening you to eternal matters and adds to you everlasting traits that never fail you.

When you experience God's presence, you not only receive blessings with value for you today, but those blessings that have worth forevermore.

Dear God, how powerfully you have blessed me. I praise you for all of the good things you give— those for now, and those that remain forevermore. Amen.

His glory is great because of Your aid;
splendor and majesty You bestow upon
him. For You make him to be blessed and
a blessing forever; You make him
exceedingly glad with the joy
of Your presence.

PSALM 21:5–6 AMP

His Goodness and His Name

Moses wanted to know God—to be in his presence and experience him personally. In fact, God was even more important to him than conquering the Promised Land.

God brought Moses into a more profound relationship by giving him a deeper revelation of his goodness. When Moses learned his name, he knew that God had honored him with an amazingly intimate understanding of his character.

> I will make all My goodness pass before you, and I will proclaim the name of the LORD before you.
>
> EXODUS 33:19 NKJV

Do you ache to know God this evening? You can know him more profoundly because he offers you a greater revelation of his kindness and nature through every situation. Just ask him to reveal himself to you. It is a request he is always glad to grant.

Dear God, more than anything else, I want to know you. Reveal your goodness and your name to me so that I may know you deeply. Amen.

The Lord answered Moses, "I will do this very thing you have asked, for you have found favor in My sight, and I know you by name."

Exodus 33:17 HCSB

Tenderly in His Arms

There are thousands of undistinguishable moments—of grazing and sleeping, of enduring the storms and natural elements, and of toilsome employments.

Yet there are also the rare, life-changing moments—of new pastures and intruders, of being lost and found, and of being born and dying.

> He tends his flock like a shepherd: He gathers the lambs in his arms and carries them close to his heart.
>
> ISAIAH 40:11 NIV

The shepherd cares for his flock in all of the moments. He knows that the drudgery of the many moments can be as difficult as the ones that turn your world completely upside down.

Whatever moment you are experiencing this evening, allow God to hold you tenderly in his arms. Thank him that the wonderful comfort of his love is available to you.

Dear God, hold me tenderly in your arms. I need the comfort of your love and of knowing you are always with me. Amen.

I the Lord your God hold your right hand; I
am the Lord, Who says to you, Fear not; I
will help you!

Isaiah 41:13 AMP

An Astounding Forgiveness

The depth of Jesus' compassion is mind-boggling. As others wrongly accused and crucified him, he recognized that they did not know what they were doing. He asked God to forgive them.

> **Jesus prayed, "Father, forgive them; they don't know what they're doing."**
> LUKE 23:34 MSG

It is an astounding, poignant picture, one that should resonate within your soul as you read this tonight.

When people hurt you, they do not understand what they are doing. They may think that they do, but they could not possibly comprehend the full ramifications of hurting someone that God loves.

So forgive as Jesus did—with compassion and understanding. Because you recognize that in doing so, you set yourself and the one who hurt you free.

Dear God, it is hard to forgive sometimes. Please give me your strength and compassion so that both of us can be free. Amen.

Be kind and compassionate to one
another, forgiving one another, just
as God also forgave you in Christ.
EPHESIANS 4:32 HCSB

The Answer Is Yes

What thought came to your mind when you read "promises God has made"? What is it that he has promised you personally?

You may be encouraged by the assurance that God will never leave you or forsake you. Or perhaps you are gladdened by the pledge that when God is your delight, he will give you the desires of your heart. Yet sometimes the promise is more personal, as when God promised Abraham a child.

> **No matter how many promises God has made, they are "Yes" in Christ.**
> 2 CORINTHIANS 1:20
> NIV

Whatever the promise is, God is sure to fulfill it. He will never forget or break his word. He will see it done in your life. Yes, he will.

Dear God, thank you so much for the promises you have made to me. I eagerly wait for them to be fulfilled—to your glory. Amen.

GOD, being the God you are, you have
spoken all these wonderful words to me.

1 CHRONICLES 17:26 MSG

He Knows Your Case

Sometimes you will be too weary to repeat your story one more time, and you will feel as if you have exhausted all of the people you usually talk to.

When it feels as if there is nobody you can confide in, remember that there is one who always listens to you. God is your excellent confidant and friend—and he already knows everything you are experiencing.

> **He always lives to speak to God for them.**
> HEBREWS 7:25 CEV

You are not alone. God is active on your behalf—helping you carry your burdens. With great wisdom, he guides you in the right course. Tonight, talk to your great and comforting God, and thank him for being by your side.

Dear God, thank you for doing so much on my behalf. My loneliness is soothed knowing you are always available to me. Amen.

We have someone who pleads with the Father on our behalf—Jesus Christ, the righteous one. And Christ himself is the means by which our sins are forgiven.

1 JOHN 2:1–2 GNT

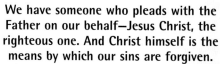

Moments of Peace
for the *Evening*

No matter how many promises God has
made, they are "Yes" in Christ.

2 CORINTHIANS 1:20 NIV

A Straight and Wonderful Path

Generally, the most expeditious way to get from one point to another is a straight line. Yet when you look on a map, highways meander around landmarks and scenery that mapmakers do their best to indicate with symbols and colors. Unfortunately, the two-dimensional nature of the map is limited in representing why the roads are built as they are.

> **Teach me your way, O LORD; lead me in a straight path.**
> PSALM 27:11 NIV

Similarly, because of your viewpoint, your life will take turns that make no sense to you. However, if you stay close to God and do as he says, you know that you are on the right road. No matter the twists and turns, you are on the straightest route to fulfilling your purpose.

Dear God, I don't understand the turns this evening, but I know you lead me in a straight and wonderful path. Help me to follow you. Amen.

Trust in the Lord with all your heart and do not lean on your own understanding. In all your ways acknowledge Him, and He will make your paths straight.

Proverbs 3:5–6 NASB

In His Name

Often the people who do not know God will have difficulty understanding why you place your confidence in someone you cannot see. They may even fear what they do not comprehend, and they endeavor to discourage or discredit you.

However, always remember that as you stand for God, he is the One who empowers and protects you. It is his duty to defend his name. And he will show himself to you in a way that both validates your trust in him and shows the one who opposes you his love.

> Help us, O LORD our God, for we rely on you, and in your name we have come.
>
> 2 CHRONICLES 14:11
> ESV

Do not fear anyone or any situation this evening. God is with you, and his name will always prevail.

Dear God, help me to love those who don't understand why I trust you. And help them to see that your name is truly great, indeed. Amen.

**Be happy and excited! You will have a great
reward in heaven. People did these same
things to the prophets who lived long ago.**

Matthew 5:12 cev

A Long-Loving God

God never delays his promises to frustrate you. Rather, he patiently waits until everything comes together and you've learned all you need to receive them.

The hope you can take from that is the absolute certainty that a pledge he has made is one he insists on fulfilling well. In other words, the blessings God gives you are yours forever—and he continues to work with you until you are ready to experience them fully.

> **The Lord is not slow about His promise, as some count slowness, but is patient toward you.**
> 2 PETER 3:9 NASB

God is committed to you for the long haul. So never fear being unqualified to receive his promises. This evening, learn from him and obey his instructions so that the waiting will be exceptionally effective.

Dear God, thank you for preparing me so well for your great blessings. Truly, you are a compassionate, wise, and long-loving God. Amen.

Beloved, since you are waiting for these, be diligent to be found by him without spot or blemish, and at peace. And count the patience of our Lord as salvation.

2 PETER 3:14–15 ESV

God Wants the Real You

Adam ate the forbidden fruit from the tree of knowledge. It was then that his eyes were opened to some undesirable elements about himself that embarrassed him. So he hid.

And though God knew where Adam was hiding, he called to him, drawing him forth in order to show Adam his love.

> **The LORD God called out to the man and said to him, "Where are you?"**
> GENESIS 3:9 HCSB

You may have some uncomfortable things deep within you that you have been concealing. Yet God wants to show you that there is no reason to keep any part of yourself a secret from him. He loves you and wants the real you.

Tonight, do not be shy. Allow God to bring you into the healing light of his love.

Dear God, thank you for loving the real me — even the hidden parts. Help me to open to you so I can fully experience your love. Amen.

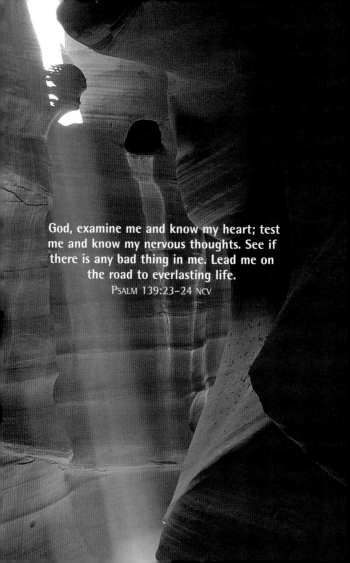

God, examine me and know my heart; test me and know my nervous thoughts. See if there is any bad thing in me. Lead me on the road to everlasting life.

PSALM 139:23–24 NCV

I Will Still Celebrate

Lift your voice tonight. Fortify yourself by singing about the goodness of God that you count on—even as everything around you seems to deteriorate.

Forget the things that are not working; they do not tell the whole story. Rather, the greater realities are his power and wisdom, which make a pleasant way for you.

Realize that the words you speak out to God in praise return to you, resonating within you to gladden your heart and lift you up.

Rejoice in God because his help is on its way and because he is invigorating you for the heights ahead. No matter what is fruitless or fails—celebrate. Surely he will help you.

Dear God, how true it is that praise delights my heart. So I celebrate you, my glorious God, for your wisdom and strength make me glad.
Amen.

The Sovereign LORD is my strength; he makes
my feet like the feet of a deer, he enables
me to go on the heights.

HABAKKUK 3:19 NIV

Preventive Encouragement

Nothing eases your heavy burdens like a friend who cheers you on and encourages you to trust in God, reminding you that he unconditionally loves you and steadfastly helps you.

Without that support, your times of waiting can seem lonely and interminable, tempting you to sink deep into doubt or turn to something other than God for comfort.

> **Encourage one another daily, as long as it is called Today, so that none of you may be hardened by sin's deceitfulness.**
>
> HEBREWS 3:13 NIV

Yet when someone who has been where you now are reinforces your faith with kind, trustworthy words, it can prevent you from losing heart.

Tonight, seek others who offer you positive, sustaining words of faith. And encourage others as well.

Dear God, thank you that encouragement has such a positive effect on my life. Please give me the words to affirm and hearten others. Amen.

Let us not give up meeting together, as
some are in the habit of doing, but let us
encourage one another—and all the more as
you see the Day approaching.

HEBREWS 10:25 NIV

Respecting God's Power

God's enormous might is sometimes shown in earth-moving events. However, the greatest display of his strength is how specifically and methodically he heals you.

This discovery comes as you humbly listen for him. He speaks a theme to your heart, and then reminds you of it through songs, Bible readings, and other people.

It is then that you realize how much more he knows about what you need than you do—and that he is gently repairing divides in your heart that were previously hidden from your notice.

> Teach me your way, O LORD, and I will walk in your truth; give me an undivided heart, that I may fear your name.
>
> PSALM 86:11 NIV

God's amazing power, then, subtly coordinates all things in order to gently heal your heart. Thank him for taking care of you.

Dear God, you truly astound me. Thank you so much for healing me so that I can praise you with my whole heart. Amen.

I give thanks to you, O Lord my God, with my whole heart, and I will glorify your name forever. For great is your steadfast love toward me.

PSALM 86:12–13 ESV

You Know for Sure

God always does precisely as he says. He has unfailingly kept every pledge to his people since the beginning, and he is doing so with you as well.

What you are not guaranteed is that God will act as you expect him to.

> **Cheer up! I am sure that God will do exactly what he promised.**
> ACTS 27:25 CEV

In fact, because he has an eternal focus, you are assured that he will accomplish his plans in a manner that exceeds your expectations. You will see your heart's desires come to fruition in a way that brings you supernatural joy and peace.

This evening, trust that God will do exactly as he promised—and that there is nothing on earth or in heaven that can stop him.

Dear God, I am certainly cheered that you will do exactly as you have promised. Thank you for giving me my heart's desires. Amen.

Your promise has been tested through and through, and I, your servant, love it dearly.

PSALM 119:140 MSG

Just Be Still

When Moses led the Israelites out of Egypt, they fled on foot as Pharaoh pursued them with his chariots and horses. To make matters worse, they found that their path of escape was blocked by the Red Sea.

> **THE Lord will fight for you; you need only to be still.**
> Exodus 14:14 NIV

Yet God supernaturally opened the way for them. They did not have to fight the Egyptians or risk drowning. They just had to obey whatever God said.

Tonight, pressures around you may be building up, and your way may appear obstructed. However, do not panic and don't do anything reckless. Rather, be still. Listen to God and wait for his instructions.

He will certainly make a way for you as well.

Dear God, thank you for making a way for me. Help me to be still before you and I will wait for your instructions. Amen.

The Israelites walked through the sea on dry
ground, with walls of water on both sides.
On that day the Lord saved the people of
Israel from the Egyptians.

EXODUS 14:29–30 GNT

Stay the Course

It is easy to be waylaid. God teaches you his truth and immediately what he shows you is challenged by what you experience and hear.

> **Keep a close watch on yourself and on your teaching. Stay true to what is right.**
> 1 TIMOTHY 4:16 NLT

It is the picture of a traveler on a straight road. There are many side roads to entice the traveler—some are easier and more pleasurable than the main road. All of them lead away from the goal, however. Therefore, the traveler must stay the course.

Tonight, examine what God has taught you, and make sure you have not been diverted from what is right by any side issues. Persevere on your journey of truth because it leads to great understanding that you wouldn't want to miss.

Dear God, please keep me from being waylaid by side issues—I want to stay true to what is right. Help me to learn your priceless truth. Amen.

You will be a good minister of Jesus
Christ, nourished in the words of
faith and of the good doctrine
which you have carefully followed.

1 TIMOTHY 4:6 NKJV

A Bearer of Good Gifts

People will often find it difficult to release the seeds God has given them specifically for the purpose of planting. However, you have seen what God does with the precious things you have given up.

> A grain of wheat that falls on the ground will never be more than one grain unless it dies. But if it dies, it will produce lots of wheat.
>
> JOHN 12:24 CEV

Like the kernel that is sown, a beautiful, nourishing harvest springs up in its place.

God took your seeds of hope and multiplied them, giving you back what you thought you had lost forever in a form that was even more pleasing.

And tonight, that is how you can comfort those who do not realize what God has given them. You can help them see that those seeds bear good gifts if they will just let them go.

Dear God, I praise you for turning my seeds of hope into a fantastic harvest of blessings. Help me tell others of your excellent gifts. Amen.

He sent me to give them flowers in place of their sorrow . . . and joyous praise in place of broken hearts.

ISAIAH 61:3 CEV

Moments of Peace *for the* Evening

The LORD will fight for you;
you need only to be still.
EXODUS 14:14 NIV

God's Greater Purposes

God changes your attitude toward everything as you walk with him. And it is an astounding thing, indeed, when God's wisdom finally makes sense to you.

The issues, people, and circumstances that brought you pain are transformed into vessels of good. They teach you to look for God's excellent purposes in even the most insignificant occurrences—knowing that they may hold some instructive glimpse of his character.

> **You intended to harm me, but God intended it for good.**
> GENESIS 50:20 NIV

This evening, you may not be at the place where you can say that God intended some difficult thing for good. However, be encouraged that the transformation he makes in you is truly worthwhile.

Dear God, I know that you have greater purposes for what I am experiencing. I thank you for transforming everything into a vessel of your good. Amen.

Just as the heavens are higher than
the earth, so are my ways higher
than your ways and my thoughts
higher than your thoughts.

ISAIAH 55:9 NCV

God Must Allow It First

Though some of your experiences come as a result of your actions and others seem to occur randomly and without sense, nothing that happens to you is a surprise to God. He knows about each event and how it will affect you.

That does not mean he chooses troubles for you; he allows them, and will most assuredly strengthen you to deal with them.

Nothing in your life is beyond God's purpose or protection. He would never allow anything that could not ultimately be used for good. Therefore, take heart this evening that even the troubles have come to you with the promise of hope.

> **When God sends us something good, we welcome it. How can we complain when he sends us trouble?**
> JOB 2:10 GNT

Dear God, I praise you that in every circumstance—whether it be a blessing or a trial—is the hope and promise of your presence. Amen.

The LORD gave and the LORD has taken away.
Blessed be the name of the LORD.

JOB 1:21 NASB

Building With Gold

Gold is beautiful, a biblical symbol of wealth and royalty. It is a rare, almost indestructible metal that is valuable wherever you go on earth.

The spiritual gold that God creates in you is faith—glowing evidence of his opulence and majesty in you. Faith is difficult to come by and valuable for this world and beyond.

> **Your faith will be like gold that has been tested in a fire. And . . . your faith is worth much more than gold.**
> 1 PETER 1:7 CEV

Like gold, faith must be purified, cultivated, and molded. Unlike gold, however, there is no way to destroy true faith. When all the brilliant metal has been consumed, faith endures.

Constructing with gold is good, but what God is building in you lasts forever.

Dear God, thank you for teaching me this evening to value faith more than gold or any other earthly valuable. Amen.

He knows the way that I take . . . When
He has tried me, I shall come forth as
refined gold [pure and luminous].

JOB 23:10 AMP

Your Priceless Character

Josiah—like many kings in the Old Testament—was not raised to honor God. His father and grandfather were evil monarchs who ruled selfishly and destructively.

However, Josiah was not confined to repeating their mistakes. He found a worthwhile example in his ancestor King David, and he sought to imitate David's superior character.

> **Josiah did what was pleasing to the LORD; he followed the example of his ancestor King David.**
>
> 2 KINGS 22:2 GNT

Perhaps you have also lacked good examples as you have grown in your relationship with God.

Take heart tonight—God has given you numerous models throughout history and in the church. Seek out God-honoring people as mentors and imitate their behavior.

Dear God, please send godly mentors for me to learn from and imitate. Thank you for providing examples of the priceless, God-honoring character that pleases you. Amen.

Be like those who stay the course with committed faith and then get everything promised to them.

HEBREWS 6:12
MSG

Dressed in His Delight

As you get ready for sleep tonight, what will you put on? Do you have some old, favorite pajamas to wear? The clothes you put on to rest are generally your most comfortable.

> **The LORD takes pleasure in his people; he adorns the humble with salvation.**
> PSALM 149:4 ESV

Likewise, dress your mind for bed by removing the concerns of the day and wrapping your thoughts in this calming truth: God delights in you. The one who protects you does not sleep, but tenderly guards you throughout the night.

Before you finally drift off to dreamland, let him know how much you appreciate his gentle vigilance. Praise him for the secure comfort that will warm you as you slumber and will faithfully cover you tomorrow as well.

Dear God, thank you for calming my thoughts so that I can sleep well. I praise you for being such a delightful and loving protector. Amen.

Let the saints be joyful in the glory and beauty [which God confers upon them]; let them sing for joy upon their beds.

PSALM 149:5 AMP

He Thinks of Everything

Count on it—there will be days when you will want evidence that God is still actively providing what he has promised you. And it will be the details of how he is working everything out that will concern you most.

> **You did exactly what you promised—every detail. The proof is before us today!**
> 1 KINGS 8:24 MSG

Your faith grows in the not knowing and by releasing all the particulars to his care. Do not fear—he has taken every facet into account and will use every hurdle to display his power.

Rest easy tonight. God has considered and taken care of details that you have never thought of. Soon enough, the proof will be before you that your faith has not been in vain.

Dear God, you know my thoughts are filled with the details. I thank you for taking care of them in such a complete and marvelous manner. Amen.

Praise be to the LORD, the God of
Israel, who with his own hand has
fulfilled what he promised.

1 KINGS 8:15 NIV

A Defender in Temptation

How do you feel when you see others struggling with the same subjects you've wrestled with? Most likely, you respond in compassion and understanding because you know how tough some subjects can be.

> Since he himself has gone through suffering and temptation, he is able to help us when we are being tempted.
> HEBREWS 2:18 NLT

This empathy develops as you grow in your resemblance to Jesus, who, being fully human as well as fully divine, experienced human temptations.

With the right focus, temptations can show how much you have become like Jesus. God's support through your trials does more than just help you pass. God helps you master the tests with humility so that you can help others overcome them as well.

Dear God, please help me to pass the tests, so that I can, in turn, help others. I want to be like Jesus more each day. Amen.

Test yourselves and find out if you really are true to your faith. If you pass the test, you will discover that Christ is living in you.

2 CORINTHIANS 13:5 CEV

Impenetrable Faith
and Love

You are a citizen of spiritual daylight. You no longer need to hide yourself or your actions in darkness where there is no real armor, only the constant threat of being revealed. Rather, because of the brightness God has given you, your impenetrable protection now comes from faith and love.

> **We belong to the day. So we must stay sober and let our faith and love be like a suit of armor.**
> 1 THESSALONIANS 5:8
> CEV

Think of that in terms of the campaigns you encounter. You do not have to rely on covert strategies in order to advance to victory. It is your trust in God and care for others that exalt you.

Tonight, embrace the new rules of engagement. Concentrate on shining goodness into other people's lives.

Dear God, please give me the armor of faith and love to honor you and care for others. May your light shine in me. Amen.

You appear as lights in the world, holding
fast the word of life, so that in the day of
Christ I will have reason to glory because I
did not run in vain nor toil in vain.

PHILIPPIANS 2:15–16 NASB

Nothing Against You

Do you know what it is like to be blamed unjustly or have things you are embarrassed about brought out into the open? It hurts to be treated in such a manner.

Yet a time is coming when no adversary will exist to harm you—God is making sure of it. He will not allow anyone to discredit you, and no one will hold anything against you. Rather, you will know what it is to be fully known and completely accepted.

> **The accuser of our brothers, who accuses them before our God day and night, has been hurled down.**
> REVELATION 12:10 NIV

This evening, imagine that day when every comment made about you is joyous and pleasing—made with love. That is the future God has for you—and that is why it is called heaven.

Dear God, thank you, that even unkind words will one day fade away. I look forward to making my home with you in heaven. Amen.

There is therefore now
no condemnation for
those who are in
Christ Jesus.
ROMANS 8:1 ESV

An Extraordinary Plan

What a happy promise—God's plans for you are exceedingly abundantly better than you can even imagine to hope for. What a glorious future awaits you.

No wonder you cannot figure out what God is doing; it is beyond conception. And so it must be in order for you to understand the quality of God's special care. Were his plans something you could dream up, they would probably be something you could achieve on your own.

> **Now to him who is able to do immeasurably more than all we ask or imagine . . . to him be glory.**
> EPHESIANS 3:20–21
> NIV

When God's plans are even more pleasing than your machinations, you realize only his love could create such an awe-inspiring future for you. Tonight, thank him for his extraordinary plans, and give him all the glory.

Dear God, I can imagine some pretty fantastic things, but your plans are matchlessly filled with love and splendor. Praise your wonderful name. Amen.

May you experience the love of Christ,
though it is so great you will never
fully understand it. Then you will be
filled with the fullness of life and
power that comes from God.

EPHESIANS 3:19 NLT

A Ready Help

The Christian life is like a deep ocean—not easily mastered, but definitely filled with profound treasures. And the many currents created between your past and God's future all allow for you to plumb the depths.

> **When you go through deep waters and great trouble, I will be with you. When you go through rivers of difficulty, you will not drown!**
>
> ISAIAH 43:2 NLT

What God is doing in you and your land-loving instincts are necessarily different, and sometimes you will feel caught in the middle of two powerful forces. However, you must allow yourself to sink deep into the waters of transformation, to the point that you feel completely inundated.

That is when God teaches you to swim. And no matter the wave that comes, you have become seaworthy and are able to survive it.

Dear God, I do prefer to stay on land—but I also realize that your waters give me true life. Thank you for teaching me to swim. Amen.

Who is mighty as you are, O LORD, with your faithfulness all around you? You rule the raging of the sea; when its waves rise, you still them.

PSALM 89:8–9 ESV

From Beginning to End

The promise that God makes a thing beautiful in his time necessarily indicates that there are unpleasant moments. Beginnings are generally tinged with some adventurous excitement and discovery, and yet they are also full of unknowns and uncomfortable adjustments.

> **He has made everything beautiful in its time.**
> ECCLESIASTES 3:11 ESV

During the middle times, mundane toil can overwhelm and dishearten. However, if the focus is God, wonderful, sustaining graces—such as patience and endurance—develop.

It is in the end—in the bittersweet of looking back—that you can see the true beauty of the journey.

Wherever you are on the path tonight, look for the beauty in it. From beginning to end, God makes it lovely.

Dear God, you know the challenges of my journey. I thank you that even this will be beautiful when you shine understanding on it. Amen.

I will bless the Lord at all times;
His praise shall continually
be in my mouth.

PSALM 34:1 AMP

He Will Show His Power

The last thing God wants is for you to become haughty while he is displaying his power in you or teaching you his awe-inspiring principles. That would be counterproductive.

> **Therefore most gladly I will rather boast in my infirmities, that the power of Christ may rest upon me.**
>
> 2 Corinthians 12:9
> NKJV

Therefore, you may often lack sufficient understanding, skill, or energy for your circumstances.

Cling to the assurance that your weaknesses are the birthplace for God's mightiest works in you. The more limitations you recognize, the more God shows his power through them.

God effectively empowers you. He is bringing you to the point where you acknowledge and embrace it so that you can fully enjoy his mighty strength.

Dear God, thank you for exposing my limitations so I can experience your strength. Truly, I can boast in my weaknesses knowing your power works through them. Amen.

I can do all things through
Christ who strengthens me.
PHILIPPIANS 4:13 NKJV

Tributes and Great Works

As you reflect on your day, you may be frustrated that it seems like only those who are dishonest get ahead. You and your loved ones are doing your best and serving God, but it appears as if only underhanded people are getting all the acclaim and awards.

However, every one of your honest dealings—every way you honor God—is recorded. Though others may not realize it, God does. And he assures you that you will be rewarded for your faithfulness.

> In his presence, a scroll of remembrance was written to record the names of those who feared him and loved to think about him.
> MALACHI 3:16 NLT

God has a better tribute for your great work. Take comfort in knowing that you will soon receive a more satisfying accolade than any you could receive from another person.

Dear God, I do get frustrated. Thank you for reminding me that you know my works and that your rewards are far better. Amen.

They'll get special treatment when I go into action. . . . Once more you'll see the difference it makes between being a person who does the right thing and one who doesn't.

MALACHI 3:17–18 MSG

The Defender of the Weak

There always will be people who effortlessly possess what you crave to receive. Whether they are strong in power, finances, beauty, intelligence, or even successful relationships, you wonder if they appreciate the blessing you would do anything to obtain.

> **The weapons of the strong are smashed to pieces, while the weak are infused with fresh strength.**
> 1 SAMUEL 2:4 MSG

You are not in a competition with them or anyone else. And although you have been denied that blessing for the moment, God knows how deeply you desire it and defends you in your weaknesses.

This evening, thank him that when you finally do receive the blessing, you will not take it for granted. You will know the true value of it and that it was God who helped.

Dear God, I thank you that even though I cannot attain that blessing through my own strength, you freely give it out of your wonderful love. Amen.

He puts poor people on their feet again;
he rekindles burned-out lives with fresh
hope, restoring dignity and respect to
their lives—a place in the sun!

1 SAMUEL 2:8 MSG

Friend of God

The book of Luke is dedicated to *Theophilus*—which, when translated to English, means "friend of God." Likewise, the whole Bible is written so that those who love God will know the hope he has provided.

> **You can know beyond the shadow of a doubt the reliability of what you were taught.**
> LUKE 1:4 MSG

Because you have a relationship with him, you know for certain that all he has taught you is absolutely factual and that you will see it proven true.

You are counted among very distinguished friends of God—such as Abraham and Moses—who also saw that his promises were completely reliable.

Tonight, realize that just as you want the best for your loved ones, so does God. He is truly a friend whose word you can trust.

Dear God, thank you for counting me a friend. And thank you for revealing the absolute certainty of your word. Amen.

I have called you My friends, because I have
made known to you everything that I have
heard from My Father.

JOHN 15:15 AMP

Believe Him

The word *faith* means that you are "persuaded of a truth." What God wants is for you to be convinced that he is real and willing to confirm his presence to you.

Without that conviction, it is not possible to please him. Think about it—how could you serve someone who you are not really sure exists? And why would you bother seeking him if you were not convinced that you would eventually find his love?

> **Without faith it is impossible to please him, for whoever would draw near to God must believe that he exists and that he rewards those who seek him.**
> HEBREWS 11:6 ESV

Tonight, you know for sure that God exists and that he is glad to reward you as you get to know him. Believe him. You will love what you find and it will please him greatly.

Dear God, I am utterly persuaded of the truth of your presence and goodness. Thank you that I have all it takes to please you. Amen.

I the LORD search the heart and
examine the mind, to reward a man
according to his conduct, according
to what his deeds deserve.

JEREMIAH 17:10 NIV

Moments of Peace for the Evening

Let us consider how to stir up one
another to love and good works.

HEBREWS 10:24 ESV

Giving in Secret

Why do you give? Have you ever considered that your charity could be a quiet act of worship? Consider being so moved by God's goodness that you give freely to another—yet give in secret, giving God the glory.

You yield what is costly to show that he is important to you. Certainly that pleases God.

Imagine what it does to the people who receive your generous gifts. Not knowing the identity of their benefactor affects them. They are beholden to none—but grateful to everyone. And they are especially thankful toward God.

> When you give to the needy, do not let your left hand know what your right hand is doing, so that your giving may be in secret.
>
> MATTHEW 6:3–4 ESV

This evening, turn your charity into an act of worship and love God by freely giving to others.

Dear God, help me to worship you through giving. Help me to see needs that I can meet in secret so that you will receive the glory. Amen.

Ascribe to the LORD the glory of His name; bring an offering and come before Him. Worship the LORD in the splendor of [His] holiness.

1 CHRONICLES 16:29 HCSB

Have You Been There?

Undoubtedly, when you were hurting, you didn't need condolences—you wanted hope. You didn't crave pity—you longed for love. You yearned for someone to reach into your situation and guarantee that it would not last forever.

He has sent me to bind up the brokenhearted, to proclaim liberty to captives and freedom to prisoners.

ISAIAH 61:1 NASB

And so, since you have been in their shoes, you know how to show kindness to those who are brokenhearted.

You recognize that the healing they need begins with friendly eyes. And you realize that the strength they need to persevere comes from an outstretched hand.

Since you have been where they are, lovingly show them where they could be going.

Dear God, you have shown me that liberty and healing are available for those who experience trials. Help me to share that wonderful truth with others. Amen.

Instead of your shame you shall have double honor, and instead of confusion they shall rejoice in their portion. Therefore in their land they shall possess double; Everlasting joy shall be theirs.

ISAIAH 61:7 NKJV

A Good Example

Paul taught the Philippian Christians to follow his example in order to lead God-honoring lives. This instruction might have appeared prideful coming from anyone else.

Those believers, however, had observed Paul in the midst of very humble circumstances—in prison and beaten. Yet they had also seen him praise God in the midst of it.

> **The things you have learned and received and heard and seen in me, practice these things, and the God of peace will be with you.**
> PHILIPPIANS 4:9 NASB

When Paul spoke of his example, he was not implying that he got everything right. Yet he was humbly dependent upon God. If others would imitate that, God would take care of the rest.

This evening, you don't have to be perfect to be a good example—you just have to fully trust and follow God.

Dear God, I want to be an excellent example—help me to honor you in all things. Thank you for taking care of the rest. Amen.

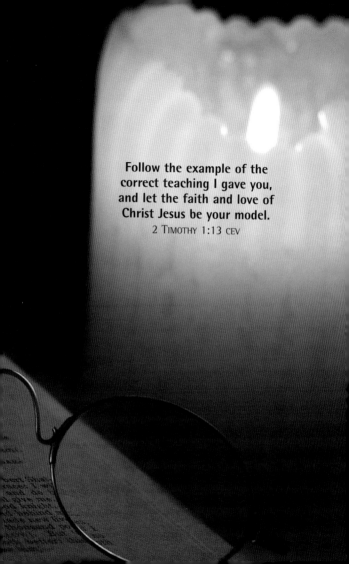

Follow the example of the correct teaching I gave you, and let the faith and love of Christ Jesus be your model.

2 TIMOTHY 1:13 CEV

Encouraging Potential

When you meet others, do you develop a vision for all they could become? Though it is often easier to recognize people's faults, it is a truly wonderful thing to identify their latent possibilities.

Scripture instructs that it is good when you stir up others to meet their potential. The idea is to put them in situations that challenge their talents and help them grow. This requires sensitivity on your part—perceiving the hidden characteristics that should be cultivated.

> **Let us consider how to stir up one another to love and good works.**
> HEBREWS 10:24 ESV

As you pray for your loved ones this evening, do you detect a greater capacity for love and good works in them? Ask God to give you a vision for drawing it out.

Dear God, please show me how to detect other people's latent potentials and stir them up to love you more and serve you well. Amen.

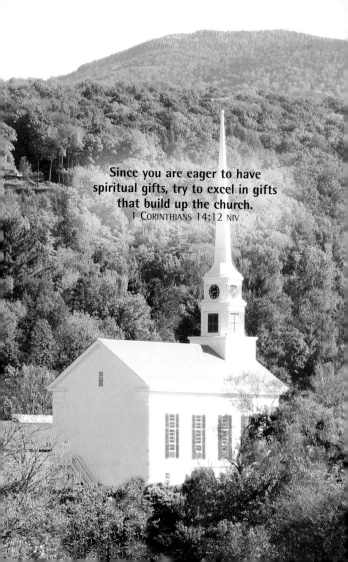

Since you are eager to have
spiritual gifts, try to excel in gifts
that build up the church.
1 CORINTHIANS 14:12 NIV

The Lord Is With You

Due to the great persecution of believers in Rome by Emperor Nero, the apostle Paul was brought to trial. And he stood alone at his first hearing because it was too dangerous for his most trusted friends to appear with him.

> **At my first defense, no one came to my assistance. . . . But the Lord stood with me and strengthened me.**
> 2 TIMOTHY 4:16–17
> HCSB

Yet God never left him—and his presence gave Paul hope.

You will encounter situations that you must face alone as well. Though loved ones will want to assist you, they will not be able to. However, you have one sure helper that stands with you through all challenges.

The Lord is with you. Rest easy tonight, knowing that his strength is more than sufficient to get you through any situation.

Dear God, thank you for being with me through everything—good and bad. I have confidence that you will strengthen me and give me great hope.
Amen.

The Lord will rescue me from all evil and
take me safely into his heavenly Kingdom.
To him be the glory forever and ever! Amen.

2 TIMOTHY 4:18 GNT

A Gentle Teacher

It is not your responsibility to make sure people act a certain way. People must choose to honor God on their own—you cannot compel them to do it.

However, you can be a good influence—your words and example can sway them in a constructive manner. Of course, attaining just the right mix of compassion and instruction may seem challenging to you. How can someone ever know just the right thing to say?

> **Preach the Word; be prepared in season and out of season; correct, rebuke and encourage—with great patience and careful instruction.**
>
> 2 TIMOTHY 4:2 NIV

Being prepared in all seasons means always listening to God and allowing him to work in you. He tempers your words and attitude. And he gives you the patience and wisdom you need.

Dear God, tonight help me to hear you so that I will be prepared to encourage and teach the people who cross my path. Amen.

Set their hopes . . . on God, who richly provides us with everything to enjoy. They are to do good, to be rich in good works, to be generous and ready to share.

1 TIMOTHY 6:17–18 ESV

An Excellent Reward

A crown awaits you, even if things are tough right now. Though perhaps you would prefer comfort to that crown, you must hold on to the hope of your kingly prize.

What does the crown signify? In ancient times, the crown was a symbol of royalty and honor—of power, provision, wisdom, and gladness. Yet this crown is better than that because it is not constructed of metal and jewels—it is made of life.

> **Blessed is the man who remains steadfast under trial, for when he has stood the test he will receive the crown of life, which God has promised.**
>
> JAMES 1:12 ESV

The excellent reward that awaits you if you remain steadfast this evening is the majestic and glorious life—full of dignity, wonder, and joy. Therefore, hold fast to the truth—for the prize is most definitely worth it.

Dear God, I praise you that there is always something better ahead—always a great hope. Thank you for the crown of life that awaits me. Amen.

The Lord, the judge who judges rightly, will
give the crown to me on that day—not only
to me but to all those who have waited with
love for him to come again.

2 TIMOTHY 4:8 NCV

Praising His Faithfulness

In writing this psalm, David envisioned God's faithfulness as so immeasurably grand that it filled all that he could perceive—to the heights of the skies. And so it is that understanding God's profound faithfulness is comparable to investigating the expansive universe.

> Your mercy and loving-kindness, O Lord, extend to the skies, and Your faithfulness to the clouds.
>
> PSALM 36:5 AMP

In learning about it, sometimes you will quickly gather facts about the millions of ways he cares for you—the countless stars he lights in your life.

At other times, you will explore some new world of closeness and will experience how sincere and profound he really is.

Therefore, this evening, praise him for teaching you the limitlessness of his faithfulness through the wonders of the skies.

Dear God, I praise you for your faithfulness that is so full of wonder. May I understand the fullness and depth of your astounding of it. Amen.

The heavens will praise Your wonders,
O Lord; Your faithfulness also in the
assembly of the saints.

Psalm 89:5 NKJV

Boundaries

Tonight, consider God's great wisdom in setting the borders of the Promised Land for the Israelites. They knew what territory was theirs to care for and defend—and how far to go without being overwhelmed by foes.

> **These are the borders of the land you are getting as an inheritance.**
> NUMBERS 34:2 MSG

Likewise, God gives you boundaries for your life and conduct. These are set before you go into situations so that your honor and person are protected.

If you set honesty as your boundary, you will not be tempted when situations lend themselves to dishonesty. Dabble in half-truths, and you may wander into precarious terrain before you even realize it.

Therefore, allow God to set your defendable borders. You will find his wisdom great.

Dear God, thank you for setting boundaries to keep me safe and honorable. I realize that your instructions and love are my greatest defense.
Amen.

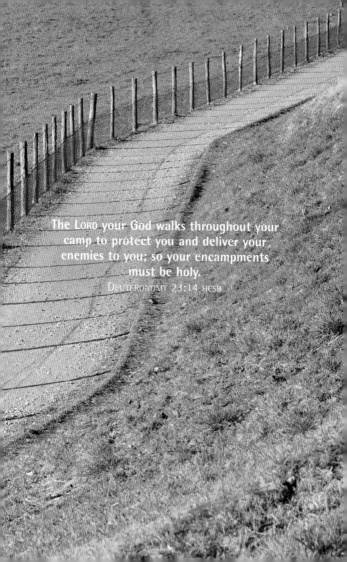

The LORD your God walks throughout your camp to protect you and deliver your enemies to you; so your encampments must be holy.

DEUTERONOMY 23:14 HCSB

His Astounding Power

It was the veil in the temple that blocked everyone's view of the Holy of Holies—the sacred place where God would meet with the high priest once a year.

One person—on only one day—had the astounding privilege of meeting face-to-face with God.

The veil of the temple was torn in two from top to bottom; and the earth quaked, and the rocks were split.

MATTHEW 27:51 NKJV

Yet when Jesus was crucified, the veil in the temple was torn in two. This symbolized the rending of everything that stood between you and God, so that you would know that you can always meet with him—every day of the year.

By his power, Jesus opened the way to the Father for you. Tonight, praise him for making your heart the new most sacred place.

Dear God, thank you for your astounding power that removes the veil and opens the way to you for me. Truly, you are wonderful. Amen.

Whenever a person turns to the Lord,
the veil is taken away.

2 Corinthians 3:16 NASB

He Walks Alongside You

God's direction for your life is not a hidden secret. You may not know where your path is taking you—or even what your next step should be—but you can be absolutely sure that what you need to know, God will show you.

Of course, there will be moments when you must ask God for wisdom. Yet experience will teach you that he is delighted when you want to do his will, and he gladly shows you what to do step by step—guiding you by walking with you.

> **The Holy Spirit whom the Father will send at my request, will make everything plain to you.**
> JOHN 14:26 MSG

God will make all things plain to you. So be patient tonight and walk with him. He will never steer you wrong.

Dear God, sometimes it's hard to know which way to turn. Yet I'm confident that you will make your path clear—so I will do as you say. Amen.

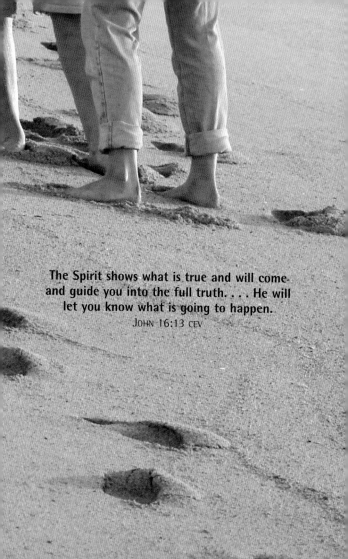

The Spirit shows what is true and will come
and guide you into the full truth. . . . He will
let you know what is going to happen.

John 16:13 CEV

The Gracious Giver

How, indeed, will God not also give you all things after such a great sacrifice? Why would he be stingy after going to such lengths to have a relationship with you?

To imagine that God is withholding some good thing is a misunderstanding of his graciousness and generosity. You can be confident that if God has not answered some dear prayer, it is either because he is perfecting it or it would hamper you from experiencing an even greater blessing.

> He who did not spare his own Son but gave him up for us all, how will he not also with him graciously give us all things?
>
> ROMANS 8:32 ESV

God loves to give to you. Therefore, praise him this evening for being glad to provide delightful things for you and that there is nothing good he is withholding.

Dear God, I know you are not stingy—but are gracious, kind, and generous. I praise you because you continue to be so good to me. Amen.

**Thanks be to God for
His indescribable gift!**
2 CORINTHIANS 9:15 NKJV

Rescued and Established

Some situations you experience will feel like quicksand. The more you try to get out of it, the deeper you sink. The more you struggle, the less you have a hold of anything solid.

Just like when you get caught in real quicksand, the best thing for you to do is to refrain from panicking. Settle down, move slowly, and call for help.

> He drew me up out of a horrible pit . . . and set my feet upon a rock, steadying my steps and establishing my goings.
>
> PSALM 40:2 AMP

God can help you get out of the mess. He can rescue you from the situation and set you in safe place. However, you must refrain from kicking and flailing about and making matters worse. Tonight, stop fighting, call to him, and relax. Help is on the way.

Dear God, only you can save me when I'm stuck. Thank you for helping me out of the quicksand. I praise your name for setting me free. Amen.

He has put a new song in my mouth, a song of praise to our God. Many shall see and fear (revere and worship) and put their trust and confident reliance in the Lord.

PSALM 40:3 AMP

The Giver of Life

It is an amazing story. God took the prophet Ezekiel from exile in Babylon to a valley filled with dry bones. The bones symbolized Ezekiel's dead hopes of returning to Israel.

God miraculously breathed life into the bones, transforming the inanimate remains. Muscles and flesh were restored, and soon, a vast army of robust soldiers stood before Ezekiel. It shocked the prophet, but he understood the application—if God could give life to those bones, he could return the Israelites to their homeland.

> Dry bones, listen to what the LORD is saying to you, "I, the LORD God, will put breath in you, and once again you will live."
>
> EZEKIEL 37:4–5 CEV

Tonight, trust God, and he will breathe life back into your hopes and dreams.

Dear God, only you can do this impossible thing. I believe that you will breathe on my situation and give life to my dreams. Hallelujah. Amen.

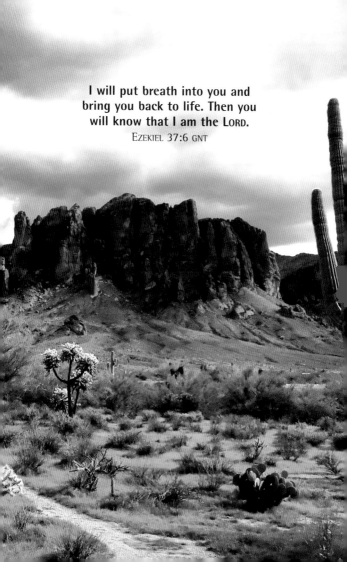

I will put breath into you and
bring you back to life. Then you
will know that I am the LORD.

EZEKIEL 37:6 GNT

Moments of Peace
for the Evening

Wait for the LORD; be strong and take heart and wait for the LORD.

PSALM 27:14 NIV

Quiet and Confident Strength

Tonight, you are challenged to do what is counterintuitive. You are to reject your anxious thoughts concerning that certain problem that has you flummoxed. You are to turn your attention from it and focus on your relationship with God.

> **Thus said the Lord God . . . In returning [to Me] and resting [in Me] you shall be saved; in quietness and in [trusting] confidence shall be your strength.**
> ISAIAH 30:15 AMP

Of course, your common sense will fight against it—insisting that you must concentrate on that critical issue. There is absolutely nothing more important than getting quiet before God.

The only answer for your agitation is to immerse yourself in God's presence. He will show you his most excellent solutions.

Dear God, please help me to be calm and focus on you. You can help me; you will make a way. Thank you for inspiring such confidence. Amen.

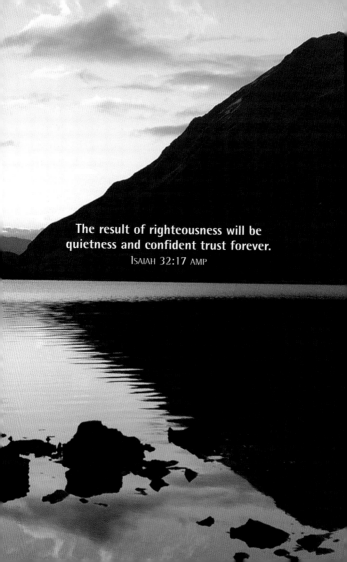

The result of righteousness will be
quietness and confident trust forever.
ISAIAH 32:17 AMP

God Has His Reasons

What was taking Jesus so long? His friend Lazarus was deathly ill, and Jesus was summoned to come quickly. Surely, Jesus could heal him.

However, Jesus waited so long that when he finally got there, Lazarus was already dead and buried.

Why the delay? Because Jesus had more glorious plans than merely healing an illness. Rather, his intention was to display the awesome power of God by bringing Lazarus back from the dead.

> **This sickness is not unto death, but for the glory of God, that the Son of God may be glorified through it.**
>
> JOHN 11:4 NKJV

This evening, you may be wondering—why is Jesus taking so long to help? There is a reason for it. Hold on just a little longer.

Dear God, knowing that you have an even greater blessing planned helps me to hold on. I look forward to seeing your tremendous power in my situation. Amen.

Jesus said to her, "Didn't I tell you that if you believed you would see the glory of God?"

JOHN 11:40 NCV

Confident Waiting

Wait for the Lord—linger a little longer for him in humility and prayer. Look for him eagerly—expect the living God to act and respond to you mightily.

Be strong—be encouraged and prevail like the soldier assured of triumph. Be firm and secure in your hope. Resolutely prepare yourself for the victory he is bringing you.

> **Wait for the Lord; be strong and take heart and wait for the Lord.**
> PSALM 27:14 NIV

Take heart—wherever your heart fails you, wherever you feel faint or fearful—allow him to support you. Exhibit determination and experience his courage as it pulses throughout your inner being—emboldening your will, mind, and soul.

Wait for the Lord—he is coming to you in strength and glory. This evening expect him.

Dear God, I do expect you. And I will wait for you with courage and determination because I know you are doing great things. Amen.

O Lord, we have
waited for You
eagerly; Your name,
even Your memory,
is the desire of
our souls.

Isaiah 26:8 NASB

Making Up Your Mind

Either God is the almighty Creator of the universe who can help you—or he is not. Either God can raise the dead and likewise bring your hopes and dreams to life—or the foundational claims of the Bible are false.

Sometimes it can feel like there is a great deal of gray area between believing God and not. However, halfway trusting him and having a backup plan usually cause more heartaches and confusion rather than peace and serenity.

> **How long will you halt and limp between two opinions?**
>
> 1 KINGS 18:21 AMP

This evening, if you have been struggling with whether to have faith in God or not, realize that it is time to make up your mind. Have confidence in God, because he has never let anyone down.

Dear God, I realize that when I doubt my circumstances, I am really lacking trust in you. Increase my faith, God. I want to believe you. Amen.

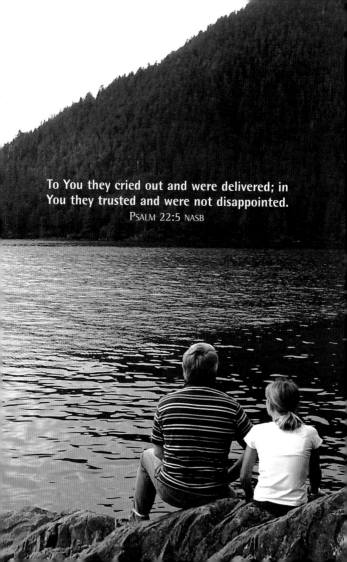

To You they cried out and were delivered; in You they trusted and were not disappointed.

PSALM 22:5 NASB

Utterly Amazing

In some ways, there is a sad lack of amazement in the world. Though interplanetary exploration and gee-whiz cinematographic advancements may briefly stir the imagination, there is a general sentiment that it has all been seen before.

> **Look and be amazed at what's happening. . . . Even if you were told, you would never believe what's taking place.**
> HABAKKUK 1:5 CEV

Part of worshiping God is standing in awe of him. Worship happens when you encounter God and realize that he is more amazing than the human mind could ever fully comprehend.

Tonight, invite God to amaze you with his presence. Allow him to astound your soul. Open your heart to him—you would not believe what he wants to show you.

Dear God, open my understanding of what it is to truly know you. Fill me with your wonder. I want to fully experience your amazing presence. Amen.

Their worship of me is made up only
of rules taught by men. Therefore
once more I will astound these people
with wonder upon wonder.

ISAIAH 29:13–14 NIV

Leave Something for Others

Harvest was a joyful time for Israel. After months of watching the crops grow, they were finally able to gather and enjoy the yield—the men cut down the stalks, and the women bound them into sheaves.

Generally, it was impossible for them to collect everything, so God instituted an interesting law: Leave something behind. This way the widows, orphans, and sojourners could find food without losing their dignity.

> **When you harvest your grain and forget a sheaf . . . leave it for the foreigner, the orphan, and the widow.**
> DEUTERONOMY 24:19
> MSG

God's desire is for his people to be generous with the less fortunate. This evening, consider: Are you kindhearted to those who are experiencing difficulties?

Dear God, you have been generous with me—help me to be so with others as well. Show me opportunities to share your love and provision. Amen.

It is good to be merciful and generous. Those who are fair in their business will never be defeated. Good people will always be remembered.

PSALM 112:5-6 NCV

He Has Given You Gifts

Though the Israelites had not yet conquered the Promised Land, God was going to teach them how to build a holy place for him—a tabernacle they could carry with them as they traveled.

How could they make such a sacred place after four hundred years of slavery? They did not have the proper training.

God filled Bezalel and Oholiab with the knowledge, creativity, and talents necessary for the task.

> **The LORD has given to Bezalel, Oholiab, and others the skills needed for building a place of worship.**
> EXODUS 36:1 CEV

Tonight, you may know of something wonderful God is doing at your church and you want to join in. Be assured that God will give you what you need to serve. Join in his activity and you will certainly have just the right gifts.

Dear God, I have been wondering if I was qualified to help in that ministry at church. Thank you for equipping me to serve you. Amen.

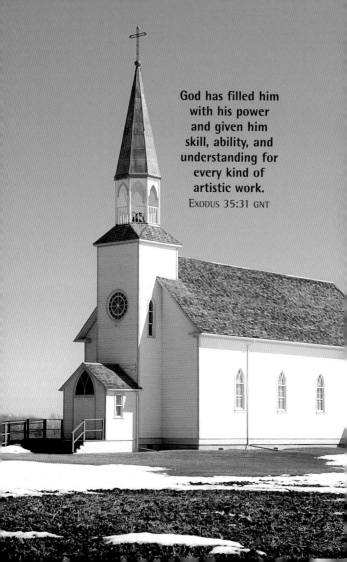

God has filled him with his power and given him skill, ability, and understanding for every kind of artistic work.

EXODUS 35:31 GNT

That Others Might Be Healed

There are still parts of the world that are very remote and difficult to get to. In fact, journeys to those places take days and only robust individuals can attempt them.

Many destinations are far easier to reach because brave adventurers forged a route and established highways for others to use.

> **"Make level paths for your feet," so that the lame may not be disabled, but rather healed.**
> HEBREWS 12:13 NIV

Tonight, realize that you can blaze a trail as well. Of course, that does not mean you construct literal roads. Rather, when you provide an example of how to go through difficulties with God's help, you create a path for others.

Because you have charted a brave course through the trial, they know the way to be healed.

Dear God, what an opportunity I have when I endure troubles. Help me to face them bravely and trust you so that others might follow my level path. Amen.

Every prudent man acts out of
knowledge . . . a trustworthy
envoy brings healing.
PROVERBS 13:16–17 NIV

His Power Fills You

Ancient clay jars may have had interesting artistic designs, but they were not generally that impressive. In fact, Paul probably chose the image of those fragile vessels because they were so commonplace. Also, they were opaque, so it was only by looking in or pouring out the contents that one could see the riches inside of them.

> We have this treasure in earthen vessels, that the excellence of the power may be of God and not of us.
>
> 2 CORINTHIANS 4:7
> NKJV

You may feel pretty ordinary tonight. In fact, anyone just glancing at you may not immediately see how special you are. However, when they get to know you—seeing what is inside and the good you do—they find that the amazing power of God fills you. You are the keeper of a glorious treasure.

Dear God, you are my treasure and I pray that people will see that the glorious power within me is from you. Amen.

Christ is in you,
which means that
you will share in the
glory of God.
COLOSSIANS 1:27 GNT

The Support of Listening

Job's friends cared about him so much that they sat with him for seven days as he suffered. They never spoke during that time. Understandably, after seeing Job experience so much pain, they did not know what to say.

Imagine sitting with someone for seven days, putting aside your responsibilities just to show your support. There is something heroic in that, in simply being there to listen.

> **No one spoke a word to him, for they saw that his suffering was very great.**
> JOB 2:13 ESV

Tonight, if you have friends who are going through tough times and you do not know what to say, it is okay. Just go to them, letting them decide when to talk and being available to listen. It will be a greater comfort than you can imagine.

Dear God, please give me the wisdom to know when to speak and when to keep silent. I pray that I may always encourage my friends. Amen.

The wisest thing you can do
is to keep quiet and listen
to my argument.

JOB 13:5-6 CEV

Worthy of Our Adoration

The law in Babylon stated that when the musical instruments sounded, everyone was to fall prostrate and pay homage to the ninety-foot gold statue. Anyone who didn't would be put to death.

> **The God we worship can save us.**
> DANIEL 3:17 CEV

There were three Jewish administrators who refused to bow. Their reason? Only the true God could save and was worthy of their adoration.

And sure enough, God delivered those three men from their death sentences in such a powerful way that the Babylonian king changed the law and acknowledged the true God.

Tonight, you may find it difficult to stand for your beliefs, but God is worth it. He will help you—just acknowledge that only he is worthy of your praise.

Dear God, only you deserve my adoration. Help me to stand firm for you, even when it is tough, because that is the right thing to do. Amen.

The Lord is great and deserves our greatest praise! He is the only God worthy of our worship. Other nations worship idols, but the Lord created the heavens.

PSALM 96:4–5 CEV

Growing in His Character

It is easy to imagine that at times the emissaries of presidents, kings, and governments get anxious. Speaking for the policies of their home nations can be difficult, even if they are not hindered by the language or culture of the country they have been sent to.

> **God has not given us a spirit of timidity, but of power and love and discipline.**
>
> 2 TIMOTHY 1:7 NASB

However, you should never be afraid of representing God. That is because you are daily growing in the character of the One you stand for, each day resembling him more and more.

The power, love, and discipline of God are making you into his well-equipped, proficient, and worthy ambassador. This evening, do not fear. Embrace the One who has transformed you into his representative.

Dear God, thank you for empowering me to be your spokesperson. I am honored to grow in your character and tell others about you. Amen.

We are Christ's ambassadors, and God is using us to speak to you. We urge you, as though Christ himself were here pleading with you, "Be reconciled to God!"

2 Corinthians 5:20 NLT

A Pleasant Harvest

Farmers undoubtedly grow weary of plowing the same land every year, especially the spots that consistently give them trouble. However, they know that if they want to see a harvest, they must do the work.

> **All discipline seems painful rather than pleasant, but later it yields the peaceful fruit of righteousness to those who have been trained by it.**
> HEBREWS 12:11 ESV

You may be experiencing something similar tonight—the plowing of territory you have been over before—repeatedly teaching you the same valuable lessons. You are assured of a good result if you persevere and trust God.

You are promised an even more pleasant harvest than the farmer, because God is growing a good character in you, and that is fruit that lasts forever.

Dear God, covering the same territory again hurts, but I know you are sowing a good character in me. Help me to persevere and trust in you.
Amen.

The fruit of the Spirit is love, joy, peace,
longsuffering, kindness, goodness,
faithfulness, gentleness, self-control.
GALATIANS 5:22–23 NKJV

The Key to the Treasure

What is it that you need to unlock all of your hidden potential and talents—to rid yourself of faults and secret hang-ups? What will open your soul to the highest and best it can be?

> **He will be your sure foundation, providing a rich store of salvation, wisdom, and knowledge. The fear of the LORD is the key to this treasure.**
> ISAIAH 33:6 NLT

Scripture teaches that the fear of the Lord is the key to your treasure. This may seem strange because fear either makes people act rashly or retreat. Yet this fear is a reverence that trusts God's intentions and fills you with confidence.

God teaches you the wisdom and courage you need in order to become all you were meant to be. He is the key to your hidden opulence, so hold him in high esteem.

Dear God, I respect your intentions and instructions. Thank you for unlocking the treasure within me, and for ridding me of all that holds me back. Amen.

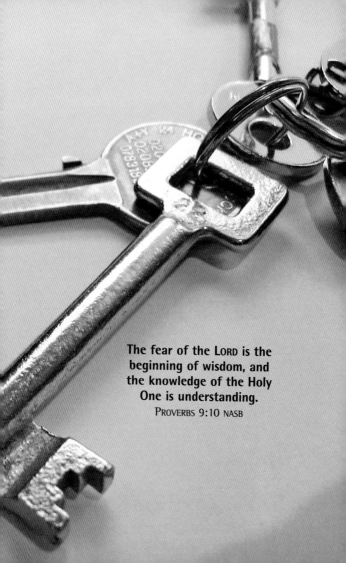

The fear of the LORD is the
beginning of wisdom, and
the knowledge of the Holy
One is understanding.

PROVERBS 9:10 NASB

Moments of Peace for the Evening

God has not given us a spirit of
timidity, but of power and love
and discipline.

2 TIMOTHY 1:7 NASB

The Alpha and the Omega

Just as the Greek alphabet begins with *alpha* and ends with *omega*, every bit of God's work originates and concludes with God himself. He created you with the ability to respond to him, and he will eventually give you a home forever.

Other good things—as you need them in increasing amounts—eventually run out. However, you cannot exhaust God. From the eternal past to an everlasting future, he freely provides you with fellowship, nourishment, and wonders to ponder.

He cares for your needs. He knows exactly what will satisfy your thirst for love and eternity. So tonight, drink him in.

> I am the Alpha and the Omega, the Beginning and the End. To him who is thirsty I will give to drink without cost.
> REVELATION 21:6 NIV

Dear God, you are my beginning and end, the only One who satisfies my thirst. Thank you for revealing yourself to me and filling my soul.
Amen.

Whoever drinks of the water that I will give him shall never thirst; but the water that I will give him will become in him a well of water springing up to eternal life.

JOHN 4:14 NASB

A Great Sacrifice

How much would you give up to love another person? More important, how far do you think others should go to show their love for you?

When you consider how Jesus left his heavenly kingdom and his majestic status to show you his love, it can be almost too immense to grasp.

> **Though he was God . . . He made himself nothing; he took the humble position of a slave and appeared in human form.**
> PHILIPPIANS 2:6–7 NLT

Yet that is the personification of great love—it gives in an overwhelming manner. It takes on limitations and gives sacrificially for the greater good of the one it loves.

Tonight, thank Jesus for surrendering everything to show his love to you. And let his example inspire you to show great love to others.

Dear God, thank you for giving up so much for me. Please help me to give sacrificially so that I may show your love to others. Amen.

Therefore be imitators of God, as beloved children. And walk in love, as Christ loved us and gave himself up for us, a fragrant offering and sacrifice to God.

EPHESIANS 5:1–2 ESV

The Joy Ahead

It will come as no surprise to you that much of your success is dependent upon your focus. However, it may astonish you that what Jesus centered on—what brought him victory—was joy.

> **Let us fix our eyes on Jesus, the author and perfecter of our faith, who for the joy set before him endured the cross.**
>
> HEBREWS 12:2 NIV

He was able to face the cross by looking past it to the wonderfully joyous prospect of offering you a relationship with God and doing God's will.

And so, knowing the delight God takes in you, be happy to fix your concentration on him this evening. Then, no matter what happens, he is the joy ahead of you. And focusing on him will give you a greater success than any other, because you will share in his certain and eternal triumph.

Dear God, when I focus on you, I center on the joy that lasts forever. Help me always to look past my circumstances to you. Amen.

Holy brothers and sisters, who were called by God, think about Jesus, who was sent to us and is the high priest of our faith.

HEBREWS 3:1 NCV

Fulfilling His Promises

Imagine Abraham sitting under the star-spotted sky, eyes twinkling with wonder, as God told him the promise. Not only would he have an heir, but he would have so many descendants that he could not count them.

> Look toward the heavens, and count the stars, if you are able to count them. . . . So shall your descendants be.
>
> GENESIS 15:5 NASB

Although he and Sarah were considerably past childbearing years, he knew God could do it. And God did. Beyond anything Abraham could have imagined.

One of the stars Abraham saw shone brightly on your behalf. As a believer, you are one of his spiritual descendants.

God is delighted to accomplish his promises for you too. So look up and rejoice.

Dear God, what a beautiful thought—each star is your pledge fulfilled. I praise you that you always do exactly as you've promised. Amen.

The Lord is near to all who call upon Him,
to all who call upon Him sincerely and in
truth. He will fulfill the desires of those
who reverently and worshipfully fear Him.

PSALM 145:18-19 AMP

Your Reason for Being

It makes sense that God would tell Moses, David, or Paul that he had raised him up for a purpose. Yet the words above were to Pharaoh, who enslaved the Israelites in Egypt. God even gave Pharaoh a chance to join him.

God has a purpose for every person, and each can choose to either accept his plans or reject him. Once your heart is willing to join him, he sets you on the path to fulfill the purpose for your being for glorifying him.

> **For this purpose I have raised you up, to show you my power, so that my name may be proclaimed in all the earth.**
>
> EXODUS 9:16 ESV

So thank him this evening, because even when you feel like you are wandering, God has placed you on the right course to accomplish what you were created for.

𝒟ear God, thank you for giving everyone a chance to join you, especially me. I want to bring you glory. Help me to please you in every way. Amen.

I cry out to God Most High, to God who fulfills his purpose for me. He will send from heaven and save me. . . . God will send out his steadfast love and his faithfulness!

PSALM 57:2–3 ESV

The Arm of God

The Bible is full of stories of underdogs who stood victoriously against mighty armies because they trusted in God. In each case, the odds were completely against them and the enemy seemed utterly invincible.

> **With him is only an arm of flesh, but with us is the LORD our God to help us and to fight our battles.**
>
> 2 CHRONICLES 32:8
> NASB

However, things were allowed to look bad in order to illustrate that there is an important factor that cannot be seen— the reality of God's help.

These numerous examples should always remind you that the clever inventions of your adversaries could never match the mighty arm of your God.

This evening, you may face conflicts that appear impossible. Yet God can easily overcome them. Line up with him on the battlefield, because he will lead you to triumph.

Dear God, I cannot see your arm, but I know it protects me. Thank you so much for giving me the victory. Amen.

He took care of them on every side.
2 CHRONICLES 32:22 NCV

Remarkable Beginnings

For Moses, life began with a death sentence. Because there were too many Israelite slaves in Egypt, Pharaoh ordered that all their newborn boys be killed.

Moses' mother hid him. And when she could not conceal him any longer, she sent him floating down the Nile in a basket, only for him to be found and raised by Pharaoh's daughter.

> **I pulled him out of the water.**
> EXODUS 2:10 MSG

Born a slave, poor Moses had great odds against him. Yet God mightily transformed him into the deliverer of Israel.

Tonight, think about your beginnings. Have you faced difficult odds? Moses trusted God, and God did the remarkable through him. Surely, God will do the same for you.

Dear God, I believe you can do remarkable things through me, though my beginnings were less than stellar. Thank you for transforming me as you did Moses. Amen.

Depend on the Lord in whatever you do,
and your plans will succeed.

Proverbs 16:3 ncv

Fragile Issues

You know how it is when you break a toe or bruise a muscle. You favor it, protect it from further injury. The same is true emotionally. You guard those areas that are hurt.

However, it is important to understand God's character when dealing with the fragile, vulnerable issues of your life. How easy would it be to finish breaking a reed that is bent in two? Or to put out a wick that is only smoldering? Most would not think twice about it.

> **A bruised reed He will not break and a dimly burning wick He will not extinguish.**
> Isaiah 42:3 NASB

God is gentle and kind—he would never hit you where it hurts. Rather, he will tenderly nurse your fragile issues so that you can be healed.

Dear God, you truly are gentle, kindhearted, and good. Thank you for treating me so tenderly and for faithfully healing my hurts. Amen.

"I will restore health to you
and heal you of your
wounds," says the LORD.

JEREMIAH 30:17 NKJV

Responding With Confidence

Job knew God. After a lifetime of seeking and serving him, he understood God's great wisdom, power, and love. And so, when trouble flooded Job's life, he was not fazed. Though he experienced pain and sorrow, he still trusted.

> **Though He slay me, yet will I trust Him.**
> JOB 13:15 NKJV

This evening, as you recline from a day of your own troubles, hopefully you are comforted by your relationship with God, by his loving character and profound wisdom. Because when you have experienced his grace, you realize that no matter what happens he will help you.

Cling to him in faith and trust. Like the gentle shepherd, he will guide you through your troubles, and your confidence in him will be strengthened.

Dear God, whether things are good or bad, I will trust you. I know that everything you allow can ultimately be used for good. Amen.

Even if I go through the deepest darkness, I
will not be afraid, LORD, for you are with me.
Your shepherd's rod and staff protect me.

PSALM 23:4 GNT

What Good Is It?

Some may suggest that to serve God, you just need to know the right thing to say. However, God never meant for believers to express their faith solely by talking about it. What good are words that are not backed with action?

Rather, just as speeches are more effective when pictures are added, your acts of kindness will lend credence to your message.

> One of you says to him, Good-bye! Keep [yourself] warm and well fed, without giving him the necessities for the body, what good does that do?
>
> JAMES 2:16 AMP

This evening, think about the people you are praying for. God may use you to answer your prayers for them. And you will see how powerful it is when your wholehearted words are backed with similarly heartfelt actions.

Dear God, I don't just want to talk about my faith—I want to live it out. Help me to be sensitive to others' needs. Amen.

I will show you my faith by what I do.

JAMES 2:18 NCV

Heavenly Greatness

What are your dreams of greatness? What is it that drives your passion to excel? Is it a title, financial endeavor, or physical goal?

Seeking such things can be consuming and exhausting—and ultimately unsatisfying. Many people have reached their goal of greatness only to find it was not all they expected. They also discovered that their fears increased. They worried that someone would surpass them, stealing the identity they had worked so hard to attain.

> Whoever practices and teaches [these commandments] will be called great in the kingdom of heaven.
>
> MATTHEW 5:19 HCSB

Jesus said that the person who teaches his principles and serves others achieves a fulfillment that has eternal significance. Work for the greatness that will never diminish.

Dear God, I want to invest my life in something meaningful that will not fade away. Thank you that everything I do in your service has rewards in eternity. Amen.

Heaven and earth will disappear,
but my words will remain forever.

MARK 13:31 NLT

Your Source Is God

You cannot be all things to all people. In fact, if you have been pulled in a hundred different directions today, and have paused for a moment of sanity—this message is for you.

Your source of strength is God. He takes care of what you cannot.

> **Our power and ability and sufficiency are from God.**
>
> 2 CORINTHIANS 3:5
> AMP

Do not get trapped by thinking that you are the only one who can save the day—that is God's job. Rather, you must stop and refocus.

Free yourself from those things that demand your attention and decide what your real priorities are, what is truly important. God gives you the strength and wisdom to handle those things, and he also takes care of the rest. Trust him.

Dear God, I confess that I am trying to fix too many things. Thank you for freeing me to care for what is really important. Amen.

Where the
Spirit of the
Lord is,
there is
freedom.

2 CORINTHIANS
3:17 NCV

A Good Gift

Your well-thought-out and instructive words could be a rare and extraordinary present to others. And this includes both words of encouragement and those of correction, given that they are said with tact and compassion.

> **A word fitly spoken and in due season is like apples of gold in settings of silver.**
> PROVERBS 25:11 AMP

Of course, as with any other gift, they are not given to draw a certain response or to flatter. Rather, they are offered out of love so that the hearer may be enriched.

The fit message is that which is both said out of love and without expectation of return. With both of these requirements met, your words will undoubtedly be a great gift to those who listen to you.

Dear God, guide my words with wisdom—out of love and without expectation of return—so that I may bless others greatly. Amen.

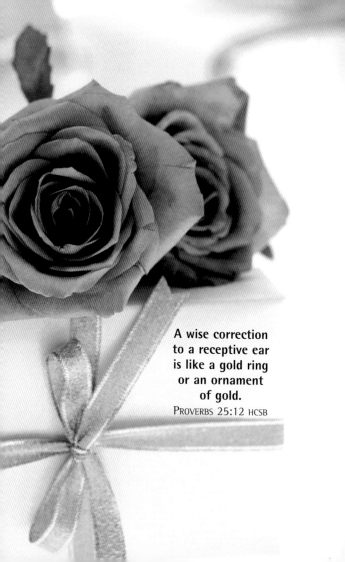

A wise correction
to a receptive ear
is like a gold ring
or an ornament
of gold.

PROVERBS 25:12 HCSB

What He Shows Through You

It is on the evenings when you feel as if your life lacks the luster it should have, or when you are overcome by the commonness of your life, that you must remember where your true brightness comes from.

> [The LORD] said to me, "You're my dear servant, Israel, through whom I'll shine."
>
> ISAIAH 49:3 MSG

If you are doing what you know is right, then you are indubitably illuminated in a manner too precious for words, because it is God shining through you.

You will not know how brightly you reflect him, because that could hinder the humble, gentle spirit he is creating in you. Yet when you are serving God, his glory radiates from you, and surely that is a light that is never overcome by darkness.

Dear God, thank you for brightening my life. Even when I feel dull, I know that your light shines through me, and that makes me glad. Amen.

I shall be glorious in the eyes of the LORD,
and My God shall be My strength.

ISAIAH 49:5 NKJV

Moments of Peace
for the Evening

[Paul wrote:] The things that you have heard from me among many witnesses, commit these to faithful men who will be able to teach others also.

2 Timothy 2:2 NKJV

He Is My Goal

The ultimate purpose for your life is not to do good works, be a good spouse or parent, or even be happy, though those are all excellent pursuits.

Your true goal is to be like Jesus, because

> **[My goal] is to know Him and the power of His resurrection and the fellowship of His sufferings.**
> PHILIPPIANS 3:10 HCSB

he meets your greatest needs and his character is the utmost goal you can aspire to. When you seek him, everything else you require is provided for you. And all your other pursuits benefit as well.

This evening, commit yourself to know Jesus and be wholly connected to him. Become like him through prayer, the life-giving truths of the Bible, and serving as he would. No other goal would do you—or him—justice.

Dear God, I want to be like you in every way. Thank you for transforming me through prayer, the Bible, and service. Amen.

I think that all things are worth nothing compared with the greatness of knowing Christ Jesus my Lord.

PHILIPPIANS 3:8 NCV

Passing the Baton

Paul had a vision for spreading the good news throughout the world. However, he knew that he could not do it alone and that its advancement could not end with his death. So he inspired others to carry on the work and train others to continue it after them. In that way, the gospel spread as wildfire sweeps throughout a forest.

> The things that you have heard from me among many witnesses, commit these to faithful men who will be able to teach others also.
>
> 2 TIMOTHY 2:2 NKJV

Tonight, you are part of something that is bigger than you are. Yet you play a critical part of its continuance. Like a runner passing a baton in a relay, you are to pass on the wisdom you received from your mentors to the next generation. So be deliberate about teaching others your faith.

Dear God, help me to teach the wisdom you've given to me. May I be a good example so that the next generation will serve you well. Amen.

He instructed our ancestors to teach his
laws to their children, so that the next
generation might learn them and in turn
should tell their children. In this way they
also will put their trust in God.

PSALM 78:5–7 GNT

Winning the Race

Certain things in life cannot be done halfheartedly. You are either committed to it, or you are not. Without passion, it is not worth attempting.

Paul encouraged believers to devote themselves to God as runners dedicate themselves to winning a race. The marathoners trained by disciplining their diets and bodies and focusing on the finish line. They did it to win, and they gave every ounce of their strength and passion to achieve the goal.

> In a race everyone runs, but only one person gets the prize. You also must run in such a way that you will win.
>
> 1 CORINTHIANS 9:24 NLT

This evening, you are challenged to commit yourself wholeheartedly to God. Train by disciplining yourself and focusing on him. With dedication like that, you are definitely a winner.

Dear God, I know I do not have to win you. However, I want to be passionately committed so that my life will honor you. Amen.

Every athlete in training submits to strict discipline, in order to be crowned with a wreath that will not last; but we do it for one that will last forever.

1 CORINTHIANS 9:25 GNT

Trusting His Hand

At times, when you are obediently in God's hand—by doing as he says—you will feel as if you are hidden by your modest circumstances. However, his hand that conceals you will also do wonderful things through you.

> **Humble yourselves, therefore, under God's mighty hand, that he may lift you up in due time.**
> 1 PETER 5:6 NIV

Remember, treasures are hidden, not things of common use. God is reserving you for special assignments and is training you through your waiting.

If you are in a humble situation this evening, take heart. It means that you are a special treasure to God and he is saving you for a very wonderful purpose. Be patient and trust the hand that hides you, for it will soon lift you to new heights.

Dear God, I trust your hand, even when I feel hidden. Thank you for considering me for such special assignments and for doing good things through me. Amen.

These trials will make you partners with Christ in his suffering, and afterward you will have the wonderful joy of sharing his glory when it is displayed to all the world.

1 PETER 4:13 NLT

Indestructible Devotion

Even in our age of advanced technological exchanges and transportation, people are parted from their loved ones for hundreds of different reasons.

Whether it be because of responsibilities, distance, problems with communication, other relationships, physical limitations, or even death, people at times encounter unavoidable barriers to being with their loved ones.

Can anything separate us from the love Christ has for us?
ROMANS 8:35 NCV

Yet you have this promise in which you can rejoice—there is nothing that can come between you and God's love. No one can persuade him to stop loving you. No limitation or circumstance can create any kind of obstacle for him, not even death.

This evening, thank God that nothing can hinder his devotion to you.

Dear God, it warms my heart to know that you are so committed to me. Thank you so much for your great, indestructible love. Amen.

I am persuaded beyond doubt (am
sure) that neither death nor life . . .
nor anything else in all creation will be
able to separate us from the love of
God which is in Christ Jesus.

ROMANS 8:38–39 AMP

Never-Ending Optimism

The last verse of the Bible is the one you read above. It closes the book of Revelation with hope, because the grace of Jesus is with all who believe in him.

It comes after the disclosure of the things that will come, of how Jesus is ultimately triumphant over evil and how his people find peace and joy with him in heaven.

> **The grace of the Lord Jesus be with all. Amen.**
> REVELATION 22:21
> NASB

And so it reveals that Jesus' grace is not merely for your troubles tonight, though it is sufficient for all of them. Rather, it inspires an optimism that literally never fails, because a wonderful eternity awaits you.

Therefore, remember that the days ahead are hopeful, for Jesus' grace is with you.

Dear God, your grace means that I share in your eternal triumph. Thank you for this unfailing hope—it will sustain me no matter what comes. Amen.

Grace to you and peace from Him who
is and who was and who is to come.

REVELATION 1:4 NKJV

Every Tear

God's delight is in giving you joy—one day taking away all of your sorrow, faults, and failures. He is providing a future free of all the painful things done to you and all the hurtful things said about you. He removes everything that separates you from Him.

> **God will wipe away every tear from their eyes.**
> REVELATION 7:17 ESV

Your body will be new, with no illness or disability. Your heart will be full, brimming with perfect happiness and eternal peace. And your mind will finally comprehend all of the things that once confounded it.

This evening, if tears are streaming down your face, close your eyes and imagine your compassionate God wiping them away. Think of the marvelous joy that awaits you and be comforted.

Dear God, I do look forward to heaven—to you wiping away my tears. Thank you so much for creating such a lovely, joyful home for me. Amen.

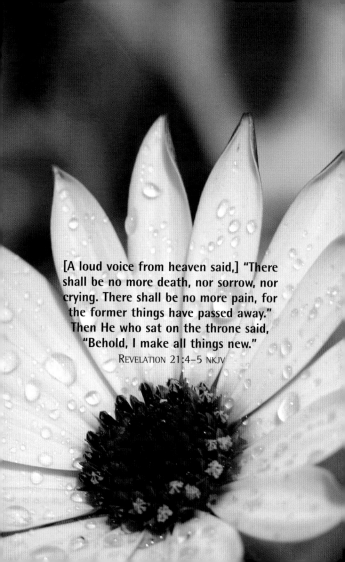

[A loud voice from heaven said,] "There shall be no more death, nor sorrow, nor crying. There shall be no more pain, for the former things have passed away." Then He who sat on the throne said, "Behold, I make all things new."

REVELATION 21:4–5 NKJV

God Knows How to Love You

There are those who tend to withdraw from others. In some ways, they do not have the energy to face other people and fear disappointing them.

On the other hand, there are those who cannot bear to sit at home. They fill their lives with activity, anxious to flee their worries and regrets.

> **They will name Him Immanuel, which is translated "God is with us."**
> Matthew 1:23 HCSB

No matter where you fall between those two extremes, God knows what you need and how to show you love. To those who withdraw, he stretches them and gives courage and acceptance. To those who cannot sit still, he sends tranquility and assurance.

Your constant friend knows how to reach you, so embrace him with all your heart.

Dear God, thank you for understanding the intricacies of my personality and how to communicate with me. Thank you for accepting me and helping me grow. Amen.

[The LORD] has said, "I will never leave you nor forsake you."

HEBREWS 13:5 ESV

Influencing the King

Who would even care about the insignificant nation of Judah? With its decimated cities and people exiled in Babylon, who would take notice of it, let alone rebuild it? The Jews in Babylon did not dare to hope of seeing their homeland restored.

> **Praise the Lord, the God of our ancestors, who made the king want to beautify the Temple of the Lord in Jerusalem!**
> EZRA 7:27 NLT

Yet when Persian King Cyrus defeated the Babylonians, God moved his heart to look favorably upon Judah. He sent resources to rebuild both the capital city and temple.

There may be something you dare not hope for tonight. Take heart that God has the ability to influence kings and any factor necessary to change your situation. From one day to the next he can restore all of your hopes.

Dear God, I praise you for having such great influence. Thank you for keeping my hopes alive and for bringing them into being. Amen.

God reigns over the nations; God is seated on his holy throne . . . for the kings of the earth belong to God; he is greatly exalted.

PSALM 47:8–9 NIV

Drawing Your Heart Back

At times, big miracle solutions inspire people to return to God. At other times, his soft voice assures believers that he is present with them. Yet one thing is sure—when he speaks, hearts are drawn to him.

> **Please answer me, so these people will know that you are the LORD God, and that you will turn their hearts back to you.**
> 1 KINGS 18:37 CEV

Though most people do not expect to hear God audibly, they long for him to respond to them, because his help, strength, and peace are all in his answers. It is the great experience of his presence that truly satisfies one's inquiring soul.

This evening, are you searching for answers? God is drawing your heart back to him through the questions. So ask and open your heart to his response.

Dear God, you are the answer to my questions. Speak to me and fill my heart, because I want to know you and love you more. Amen.

Let me see your face, let me hear your voice; for your voice is sweet, and your face is lovely.

SONG OF SOLOMON 2:14 AMP

Since You Asked

There is nothing that can cause anxiety like silence. You pray to God with faith and passion about something dear to you, and then you hear absolutely nothing. Soon your hope begins to fade away.

> **Don't be afraid! God has listened to your prayers since the first day you humbly asked for understanding, and he has sent me here.**
> DANIEL 10:12 CEV

Yet God heard you and has been preparing an answer since the first moment you prayed. Just because there is no visible evidence of his work in your situation does not mean he is ignoring you or has rejected your request.

On the contrary, he has taken your pleas to heart and is working diligently to provide what you need. This evening, do not despise or fear the silence, because God is most certainly sending his answer.

Dear God, thank you that your silence does not mean that you have rejected my request. I continue to expect your answer with great hope. Amen.

The LORD has heard
my cry for help;
the LORD will
answer my prayer.
PSALM 6:9 NCV

So Many Times?

Naaman had leprosy, a painful and disfiguring disease. Feeling hopeless, he went to a prophet to be cured. However, the prophet told him that he would have to wash in the Jordan River seven times to find relief.

> **Go wash and be cured.**
> 2 KINGS 5:13 CEV

Why seven times? Can't you just cure me? Tonight, you may be wondering why God has made you focus on the same hurt area of your life so many times. Can't he just heal you?

Yet just as Naaman showed faith by going to the Jordan seven times and was cured, you must have faith as well. God knows what he is doing, and he will heal you. Trust him, no matter how many times it takes.

Dear God, sometimes I think, Not one more time. But then you help me through and give me even deeper peace. Thank you for healing me. Amen.

We're not quitters who lose out.
Oh, no! We'll stay with it and
survive, trusting all the way.

HEBREWS 10:39 MSG

With Outstretched Arms

After great victories, defeats, and even during times of waiting, you will sometimes feel far from God, perhaps even unworthy of his presence.

It can happen when you have not spent any time with him. Sometimes you will feel that way when you have been serving him faithfully, but the work has replaced him as your focus.

> **Where could I go from Your Spirit? Or where could I flee from Your presence?**
> PSALM 139:7 AMP

Yet no matter how far from God you feel, he is really only one turn away—the move your heart makes back to him. His arms are always outstretched toward you, and he wants you to realize that he always wants you back.

Tonight, run to his open arms. You'll be glad you did.

Dear God, thank you for being near even when I feel far away. Please keep me close to you and safe in your arms always. Amen.

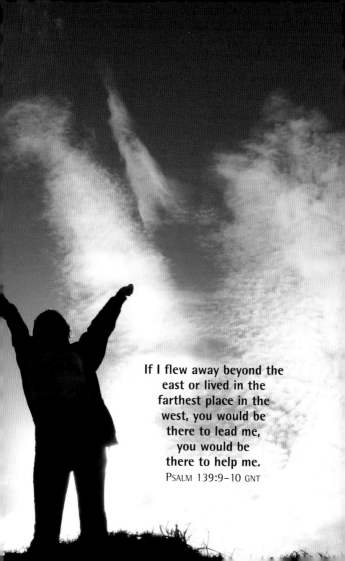

If I flew away beyond the
east or lived in the
farthest place in the
west, you would be
there to lead me,
you would be
there to help me.
PSALM 139:9–10 GNT

Support and Understanding

Naturally, the disciples did not want Jesus to face the pain and humiliation of the crucifixion. They wanted to protect him, even to fight for him, if necessary. Jesus knew that in order to have a resurrection, there had to be a crucifixion.

> **How then would the Scriptures be fulfilled that say it must happen in this way?**
>
> MATTHEW 26:54 NIV

Needless to say, you will not want to see your loved ones go through difficult circumstances either. However, God is surely accomplishing something important through their trials, even if you cannot see or understand it.

This evening, show them your love and help by supporting them. In that way, you make things easier for them in a meaningful way, and God's purposes for them are fulfilled.

Dear God, I don't understand the reason for my loved ones' troubles, but I trust you. Please help me to be a strong and gentle support. Amen.

**A friend loves at
all times.**
PROVERBS 17:17 NASB

I Want to Know You

No person can think as God does. His thoughts are so different and far above what is humanly possible—there is simply no way to figure him out.

Yet it is possible to be so close to him that you are united in purpose with him. That is achieved through the daily disciplines of prayer, Bible study, and obedience. Through them, God reveals his infinite mind to you in ways you can comprehend.

> If you are pleased with me, teach me your ways so I may know you and continue to find favor with you.
>
> EXODUS 33:13 NIV

You desire to know God, and he wants to teach you his ways and transform your thoughts to be consistent with his. This evening, stop trying to figure out what he is thinking and simply endeavor to know him.

Dear God, I do want to figure you out, but most of all, I just want to know you. Thank you for teaching me your ways. Amen.

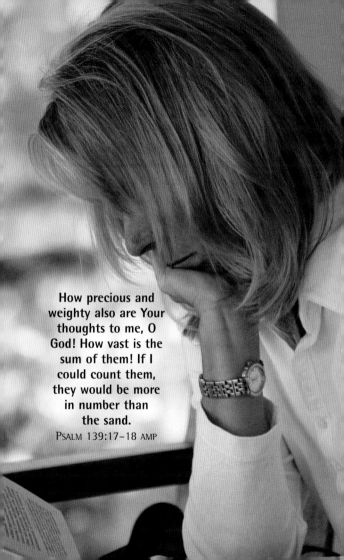

How precious and weighty also are Your thoughts to me, O God! How vast is the sum of them! If I could count them, they would be more in number than the sand.

PSALM 139:17–18 AMP

Influencing Those Around You

It has been said that the greatest love anyone can show to another is to give his life for him. Most people would like to say that they love so deeply.

Unfortunately, many do not recognize that the assignment of laying down one's opinions for their loved ones—though less dramatic—is equally important.

> **God's servant must not be argumentative, but a gentle listener and a teacher who keeps cool.**
> 2 TIMOTHY 2:24 MSG

Even skilled debaters may alienate their audience instead of winning them over.

The gentle, kindhearted listener most often influences those around them. This evening, that is precisely the type of person you are challenged to be.

Dear God, please help me to be a good listener. Help me to understand where people are coming from so that I can gently lead them to you. Amen.

Be humble when you correct people who oppose you. Maybe God will lead them to turn to him and learn the truth.

2 Timothy 2:25 CEV

A Reason for Confidence

There will be times when circumstances temporarily draw you away from the one thing that you are most committed to—the person, project, or issue that has most required your attention.

> Let him who boasts boast in this, that he understands and knows me, that I am the LORD who practices steadfast love, justice, and righteousness.
>
> JEREMIAH 9:24 ESV

It will be hard to let your responsibility go, even for a short time. Yet you are confident because God cares about what you care about. You need to acknowledge that he is ultimately the One in control of your situation.

Tonight, know that everything is going to be okay. You leave your precious concern in the very best hands—his hands. So let go and have confidence that the almighty God tenderly guards that which you love.

Dear God, thank you for caring for my concerns. Please help me to let go and trust you. Truly, I have no reason to worry. Amen.

Blessed is the man who trusts in the LORD, whose confidence indeed is the LORD. He will be like a tree planted by water. . . . It will not worry in a year of drought or cease producing fruit.

JEREMIAH 17:7–8 HCSB

The Praiseworthy Perspective

Thomas à Kempis wrote, "Great peace is with the humble man, but in the heart of a proud man are always envy and anger." Though envy and anger are motivating forces, they are more destructive than constructive. It is tough getting anything beneficial done when you are constantly focused on gaining advantage over others.

> **Don't be jealous or proud, but be humble and consider others more important than yourselves.**
> PHILIPPIANS 2:3 CEV

Tonight, concentrate on building others up and bringing out the best in them. Because when you identify their positive traits and cheer for their success, you help them to grow in their God-given purpose. Certainly, that is always a constructive and praiseworthy pursuit.

Dear God, help me to humbly see the best in others and challenge them to grow, so that they will be encouraged and you will be glorified. Amen.

The reward for humility and fear of the
LORD is riches and honor and life.
PROVERBS 22:4 ESV

Moments of Peace for the Evening

Let him who boasts boast in this, that he understands and knows me, that I am the LORD who practices steadfast love, justice, and righteousness.